Journey From Lack
to Radical Generosity

A STORY THAT NEEDS TO BE TOLD

BECKY
SWANSTRUM

Scriptures marked AMP are taken from the AMPLIFIED® BIBLE, Copyright ©2015 by The Lockman Foundation. Used by permission.

Scriptures marked AMPC are taken from the AMPLIFIED BIBLE (AMP), Copyright © 1954, 1958, 1962, 1964, 1965, 1987 by the Lockman Foundation. Used by Permission.

Scriptures marked ESV are taken from the THE HOLY BIBLE, ENGLISH STANDARD VERSION® (ESV), Copyright© 2001 by Crossway, a publishing ministry of Good News Publishers. Used by permission.

Scriptures marked KJV are taken from the KING JAMES VERSION (KJV), public domain. Scriptures marked NAS are taken from the NEW AMERICAN STANDARD® (NAS), copyright© 1960, 1962, 1963, 1968, 1971, 1972, 1973, 1975, 1977, 1995 by The Lockman Foundation. Used by permission.

Scriptures marked NIV are taken from the THE HOLY BIBLE, NEW INTERNATIONAL VERSION ® (NIV), Copyright© 1973, 1978, 1984, 2011 by Biblica, Inc.™ Used by permission of Zondervan.

Scriptures marked NKJV are taken from the NEW KING JAMES VERSION® (NKJV), Copyright© 1982 by Thomas Nelson, Inc. Used by permission. All rights reserved.

Scriptures marked NLT are taken from the HOLY BIBLE, NEW LIVING TRANSLATION (NLT), Copyright© 1996, 2004, 2007 by Tyndale House Foundation. Used by permission of Tyndale House Publishers, Inc., Carol Stream, Illinois 60188. All rights reserved. Used by permission.

ISBN 978-1-7373597-0-8 (paperback)

ISBN 978-1-7373597-1-5 (ebook)

CONTENTS

INTRODUCTION

The first thought of writing this book came when I applied to the brand-new Bethel School of Supernatural Ministry online program (BSSM-O) in June of 2020. Throughout the years, I have watched God bring hope and increase into my financial situation, and as I put God's stewardship principles to work in my life, I saw God work in amazing ways. Once I got married, my husband Clint and I worked together to become extremely generous givers. Over the years, I shared my and our journey with many young people; college-aged broke students, deeply-in-debt-upon-graduation college students, and struggling young families. Meanwhile, we were inching along trying to finish well.

Then in June 2020, as I was sharing my story in my BSSM-O interview, the woman who was interviewing me asked me if I had ever considered writing a book. No, I hadn't. But something was birthed in me and I thought perhaps I should at least try. It would be much easier to hand someone a book than to spend hours talking about our journey. Most people don't have hours to sit and listen. So the seed was planted.

The other day, song-writer and storyteller Ray Hughes posted this on Facebook and it shows perfectly the motivation in my heart as I write my stories:

"As long as words have been spoken, stories have been told … As long as children are born, we must tell the stories. Otherwise, they will listen to a world that has ceased to care enough to remind them of who they really are. Today is a good day to tell a story that shows them where dreams come from and what hope looks like … This isn't a five-year plan, it's a 500-year vision. Your stories should be gently waking the boldness in those that will sing tomorrow's hopes and dreams. The world needs tellers, be a teller today. Tomorrow needs your story." (Hughes October 12, 2020)

And from Bill Johnson, pastor of Bethel Church, I found my purpose in writing these stories of God in my life:

"The testimony of God creates an appetite for more of the activities of God … The simple act of sharing a testimony about God can stir up others until they expect and see God work in their day." (Johnson 2013)

My hope is that as I share my God-stories and the lessons I have learned, that the path I have taken will inspire you to take the steps to finish well while touching and blessing the world around you. I truly believe that God is no respecter of persons and that what He has done for me, He is willing and eager to do for you. He loves weaving His plan throughout our lives. Do it again, God! Do it again!

Chapter 1

THE BEGINNINGS

I don't remember how old I was when I first recognized lack. Probably pretty young. I remember every house we lived in from the time I was two years old. I never knew the houses were rentals or had any understanding of what money was or where it came from to pay for these houses. I certainly had no understanding of the monthly expenses of living that I now do as an adult. My dad was a school teacher with a low salary. He drove a school bus on the side and volunteered as a pastor of a small community church in the San Bernardino mountains of Southern California. Even though money was tight, I didn't know that until sometime in elementary school. I was blissfully ignorant, having plenty of everything I needed: shelter, food, and family.

I have a photograph of me when I was three years old. It is one of my favorites. I was standing in a neighbor's driveway in Valley of

Enchantment, California. I had a little winter glove on my right hand and I was holding my hand out tentatively. The neighbor had been coaxing me to feed the chickadees. He had put some bird seed in my hand, and there I was with a little bird perched on my little hand. I look at that picture and see a sweet, tender-hearted, gentle little girl with great trust in her heart. A happy-hearted little girl blissfully unaware of the stress and sorrow in the world, not yet having the walls up that would protect her from the perceived and real dangers of the world to come.

But the sense of lack had already begun creeping in. My mom was a great cook and we ate really good meals at home, but the special joy of eating out at a restaurant was non-existent. When we did have food that wasn't homemade, we kids wouldn't have a whole meal to ourselves. We had to share and split meals. We would get take-out hamburgers on special and each of us might get half a hamburger.

I do remember one significant sit-down meal in a restaurant. One summer when we were in Arizona visiting my great Aunt Alice, my mom's cousin Tom took us to a steakhouse. It was such a wonder being in that place. I still remember the big wooden tables, the benches, and the cool darkness inside. Tom was very wealthy and was treating us, but mom and dad ordered one plate of dinner for us four kids to split. I was so disappointed. My mom and dad got steak, but for some reason my parents felt we wouldn't appreciate it, so the four of us split a hamburger and fries. I felt devalued, unimportant, and so sad. I longed for something better, for no fear, and the freedom to enjoy the good things that God seemed to offer.

Each Christmas Aunt Rose from Buffalo would send my two sisters and me brand new store-bought dresses. My favorite was a red, brown, and orange dress with fall leaves and two tiny acorns on the lapel. I felt so pretty in that dress! I loved those store-bought dresses even though Aunt Rose strategically bought them at least one size too big so it would take the whole year for us to grow into them. It took some time before I realized that it was normal for many of the kids I went to school with to have all their clothes store-bought. Our family had hand-me-downs and clothing my mom and older sister sewed. I felt so awkward in those home-made clothes, which I was wearing in many of my annual school pictures. I never shared those pictures and ended up throwing most away, always putting on a brave face, keeping those walls up so no one would know that I knew I didn't really fit in.

A BIT OF FAMILY HISTORY

My mom had come from a wealthy lineage. Her father, my grandfather Henry Guernsey Hubbard, was the youngest of four children. Long ago, his parents and relatives had homes in Martha's Vineyard, an island located south of Cape Cod, Massachusetts known for being a popular summer vacation area for the wealthy. A book, which documents the history and genealogies of my mother's side of the family, *One Thousand Years of Hubbard History, 866 to 1895: From Hubba, the Norse Sea King, to the Enlightened Present,* (Day 2016) had been passed on through the family, and we saw it often. My grandfather's brothers made great wealth, one as a geologist, another as an entomologist and horticulturist who had displays in the Smithsonian Museum. At some point, the family moved to Detroit, Michigan and became prominent, wealthy, and influential there. My mom's father never made it into the massive wealth and fame his grandfather, father, and brother attained. My mother always felt that this wealth should have been hers and she was very vocal about that.

My father, on the other hand, had parents who were poor immigrants from Germany. He was their first child born in America and came from a very godly line. But his family didn't have much wealth. His dad was a baker in Buffalo, New York, who moved his family to Los Angeles, California after he suffered a fall off a ladder and sustained a back injury. When my dad was in his late teens, his father passed away from a botched blood transfusion while in surgery for his back. My dad did his best as the oldest son in the family, obtaining his degree and becoming a teacher, trying to be a good son to his mother and a good sibling to his younger brother. He then met my mom in L.A., and they soon married.

Within two years of mom and dad marrying in their early twenties, they had my sister, then me twenty-one months later. The greatest legacy they gave me was not wealth, but a love for Jesus and the Word of God. During these younger years, I knew I was loved by God more than He loved the sparrows. A favorite Bible passage was Matthew 10:29-31 where Jesus said, *"Are not two sparrows sold for a cent? And yet not one of them will fall to the ground apart from your Father. But the very hairs of your head are all numbered. Therefore, do not fear; you are of more value than many sparrows"* (NASB). I loved that He knew how many hairs were on my head and that He also kept my tears in a bottle

(Psalm 56:8). I loved the song, "His Eye Is on the Sparrow" because I needed to know He cared for me.

We lived in Norwalk, California (near L.A.) when I was really young. I remember when I was around two years old coming into the living room where mom and dad were sitting. My older four-year-old sister had come up with a plan to sing the little song, *Teensy Weensy Spider*, and act it out for mom and dad. There was joy in the room, excitement, love, and acceptance with lots of fun and laughter at that moment. I felt loved and cherished. How I loved those family times.

When I was in elementary school, we moved to the mountains where dad taught and took on pastoring the little church. For a couple years, we lived in a house that was in a residential area behind my elementary school. My kindergarten teacher, Mrs. Tone, was always draped in big, flowing, purple dresses. I remember the room, the desks, the area where we sat and listened to stories and did music marches with musical instruments, our cubbies, and our little napping cots. I remember playing in the playground and chasing the boys. I was fearless and tough–definitely a tomboy at heart. Mrs. Tone told my mom and dad that I chased boys, though, and I got in trouble for that!

There were so many little mountain communities in the San Bernardino mountains, and we were familiar with all of them. As we drove from Valley of Enchantment to Cedarpines Park where we later lived, we would pass a small amusement park that had four rectangle trampolines. I had such a desire in my heart to jump on those trampolines. I would look longingly at them, and I asked once or twice if we could go there, but our family did not have money to spend on "frivolous things" and entertainment like that. There were no movies, no ice skating, and no theme parks in our world.

FAMILY TIMES

Our family did lots of traveling–to the Grand Canyon, Yosemite, the California coast and tidepools, the redwoods, both the coastal and the giant ones–all over the state. As part of dad's continuing education requirements as a teacher, he would need to take summer courses in various places. Our family would spend weeks on the road and, because we had no money for hotels, we would camp out. We were like hobos all packed into our tan Chevy carry-all with tents, tarps, cots, and even an old fire pit camp oven. We were usually camping somewhere for my August birthday, and mom used that old camp stove to bake my special birthday blueberry muffins many times. We had such good camping family times. Mom always had a load of food in the ice chest. On the road to our destination, we would pull over into a rest stop, put the tailgate down, and make our sandwiches. We even had the "slop bucket" (potty can) in the car for those inevitable mid-transit needs.

In 1966, when I was going into seventh grade, we took a road trip across the United States, visiting friends as we made our way to Buffalo, New York, where my dad was from. We went in our "carry-all" with a big mattress in the back where we kids were during the trip. As we stopped in each state, we had a bit of spending money we had saved to buy souvenirs. Our favorite little items on that trip were small ceramic animal "families." I bought a family of skunks, kitties, boxer dogs and many others. It was such a delight to have my little animal families to play with across the country. At Aunt Rose's house in New York, one of my baby boxer dogs rolled under the freezer in the play room and I couldn't get it back. I was so disappointed that it was never recovered. I still have these little relics of my past and remember the joy they gave me in my small world.

On our way back to California, we drove across Canada. It was important to dad and mom that every Sunday we were at church, so we would drop in on these little community churches across the country. As a young pre-teen, it was so difficult to step into these unknown churches with unknown people and attend Sunday School class with the few kids who lived in the community. I didn't have great social skills–it just wasn't something that was taught in our home. Perhaps my parents thought we would just know how to act in social situations. We didn't. Or at least I didn't. I felt shy, awkward, and different. It was very uncomfortable, and I don't think any of us kids particularly enjoyed it.

One big memory of this trip that directly relates to my understanding of finances and feeling lack was that the carry-all broke down in some little Canadian town. We had to have it towed, we spent an unplanned night in the town, and there was just a swirl of fear surrounding this event. As always, the theme of not having enough to pay for this extra expense dominated. There was always an underlying cushion of fear and anxiety.

AUNT ALICE

A delightful part of every summer was when we got to go to Oracle, Arizona, to my great Aunt Alice's place. She lived in the desert amid the rattlesnakes and scorpions on a small "compound" with her main house, a guest house and a wonderful, small swimming pool.

Aunt Alice was my mother's aunt and perhaps my mom's favorite person in the world. When we were at Aunt Alice's every summer, I knew we would be well taken care of. She always stocked the refrigerator with all our favorite foods that we never got at home – soda pop, Fiddle Faddle, and even Partridge Farms cakes! It was glorious. She was a servant who loved us and blessed us with what she had. She was well-known in the community, a home-grown archeologist of sorts who would take us on "digs" into the desert to find pottery and other Anasazi treasures. Even though Aunt Alice lived very simply, she had no fear of lack. She was generous and kind. Her generosity made an impact on me that still affects me to this day. Seeing how she recognized our preferences, even as little kids, that she enjoyed serving us, and loved us well made a big impression on me and opened up my heart to do that for others.

Aunt Alice cherished all creatures from the chickadees and cottontail rabbits to her two little old dogs. They were half blind, deaf, and followed her everywhere. Her love of animals extended to every living thing. She instilled that love in my mother, who then extended it to us.

One year we were able to take our horses down to Oracle for the summer. Aunt Alice put together a small make-shift corral and my sister and I spent many glorious hours riding, exploring the Arizona desert, avoiding diamond back rattlers, being wild and free. It was something my mother used to do as a nineteen-year-old when she lived with Aunt Alice for a year.

In looking back to times like this, it is clear to see that even though we had lack in some areas, we also enjoyed the blessing of the Lord on our family. I am sure this is because of the legacy we had through my dad's family–a family who honored God, tithed, and served Him throughout the years. Our family may not have had the best, but we always had enough. We always had something extra that God gave us for His and our mutual delight–animals being a huge part of that and bringing all of us great joy.

At home, we had horses, ponies, and other critters around us at all times. Animals were a major part of our world. Several of our cats were named Fritzy. First it was Fritzy I, then when he ran off, we had Fritzy II, Fritzy III, and so on. The cats would get tired of little girls giving them baths and dressing them in doll clothes and eventually disappear. We also always had a beloved dog–King, Coby, Joel, Caesar–and more. There were chickens and rabbits, too. Some were for pets, some for eating. Butchering day with the chickens was always exciting. My Aunt Martha, mom's sister, would arrive and she would get a big pot of water boiling. As soon as the chickens were butchered, they would be dunked in the water and defeathered easily. I never had to do any of the work on those days, but it was always so exciting and interesting to watch. Not your average family, for sure!

A SINGING LEGACY

Our family sang together a lot. There were many car trips filled with the little Bible choruses and songs that we all loved. The harmonies my dad and mom had together were beautiful. My earliest memories as a two-year-old are of singing my favorite song with my mom:

"When you feel downhearted, cheer up, cheer up!
Remember to sing and to pray
The Lord sends the rainbow to follow the rain
So, cheer up, cheer up, cheer up … cheer up!"

The Word of God was of utmost importance to them, and they passed that on to us. Every Sunday afternoon we would come home from church, have lunch, then sit at the table where dad had rolled out a huge piece of blank newsprint. We would spend the next hour writing out our Bible verses from the little books we had from our Bible Memory Association program. Once a week we would recite our verses to a leader and earn little prizes. The Word in me is my lifeline to heaven and the heart of God! It was all started and built upon at a young age. Oh, how I love the Word and am grateful for this legacy my parents gave me. It is a strong truth that rings in my heart, *"For the word of God is quick, and powerful, and sharper than any two-edged sword, piercing even to the dividing asunder of soul and spirit, and of the joints and marrow, and is a discerner of the thoughts and intents of the heart"* (Hebrews 4:12 King James Version).

We went weekly to Good News Club where we sang songs about Jesus and learned the stories of the Bible via flannelgraph–the flannel covered board where felt-backed cardboard Bible characters were placed to create the story. The Old Testament people were my favorites. I connected and related to them and wanted to be like them in every part of my life. I would come home and set up chairs in a half-circle, get my mom's flannel graph board out and "teach" the Bible lessons to my little group of empty chairs. I loved Jesus and His Word and wanted to follow Him all the days of my life.

Prayer was also a priority in our home. My dad was the spiritual leader without doubt. Always before bed, he would gather us and we would pray in order, from youngest to oldest. I have to admit sometimes I would fake being asleep when it came to my turn as I was third in the lineup of six and couldn't think of anything to pray or was just too tired to pray that night.

Every trip we would ever take, after we were all packed in the car, before we would move an inch, dad would pray over the trip, over us and the journey. It was a safe place to be. It was a wonder having a dad who believed God and put Him first and foremost. This left a deep and lasting impression on my heart.

ENOCH

As I mentioned, the Old Testament Bible people were my favorites. They were my friends. We didn't watch much TV in our house, but we did have Moody Bible Institute film strips on all the Bible characters. The feats of faith they did framed my world. I especially loved Enoch and wanted so badly to be like him. *"And Enoch walked with God: and he was not; for God took him"* (Genesis 5:24 KJV).

I would spend hours studying them, thinking and dreaming of the exploits I would do with Deborah, Gideon, Elijah, Elisha, Joseph, and Enoch. They were more real to me than the people in my world. They inspired me and gave me hope that God's plan for my life was just as big, just as important, just as mighty as these amazing people. I knew that they were alive and I wanted to do exploits just like them.

A DIFFICULT LESSON IN GIVING

I often heard, especially from my mom, the verse, "*It is more blessed to give than to receive*" (Acts 20:35 KJV). Mom often used scripture verses to "motivate" us into behaving. It felt like guilt. Another was "*The laborer is worthy of his hire*" from I Timothy 5:18 (ASV). We heard this one whenever she was eating some tasty snack, but there wasn't enough for us and she didn't want to share. She let us know that because she had cooked it, she could have it.

As far as giving goes, it has taken me years to really believe and experience the truth about giving and receiving. I certainly didn't enjoy hearing Jesus' words throughout my childhood, though. They seemed like another scripture mom used to achieve her end goals, whatever they might have been.

One Christmas, I received the most amazing gift from my grandpa. It was a toy ship–a twenty-seven-inch Texaco SS North Dakota Toy Model Tanker Ship. It was so beautiful! I loved my ship and would take it out after a rain to float in the mud puddles. It meant the world to me. My cousin Tommy, who lived in Washington, got the identical toy for Christmas from Grandpa. I'm sure he loved his ship as much as I loved mine. One day, tragedy struck his family and their house burned down. I don't remember much of the circumstances surrounding it all, but I do remember that my parents approached me and asked me to give my Texaco tanker to Tommy. It was a horrible decision for an eight-year-old to make. This was something I so loved and that fit my personality so well, and I had to give it up. I don't think I was forced to give it, but the guilt I experienced with the thought of NOT giving made a deep and lasting impression. So my ship was sent off to Tommy. I did not feel the release and joy of it being better to give than to receive. It would take me years of more giving, strategic giving, purposeful giving, to come into an understanding of what Jesus meant. In fact, I think that being pressured to give that boat put me back a few steps in being willing to launch out and try to give with a thankful and joy-filled heart. Life was all about holding tightly to what I had and keeping safe with all my walls and boundaries strong and secure.

R.G. LETOURNEAU

During some of my earliest years, my dad was completing his higher education schooling. He had a beautiful oak tool box with lots of drawers and intricate mechanical tools. I was fascinated with it and heard him talk from time to time about where he had gotten it. From what I remember, he had attended one year at LeTourneau University, an interdenominational Christian polytechnic university based in Longview, Texas. My dad was interested in engineering and started through the program.

The founder, R.G. LeTourneau (1888-1969), has a fascinating testimony of being a business magnate, philanthropist and inventor who wanted to serve God. He was counseled that God not only needs missionaries who go to the world and preach the gospel, but God also wanted business people who would bring Him into the business world. R.G. decided to "stay" and invest himself in the business of building earthmoving equipment. He was invited into and accepted God as a partner in his business. He was totally sold out and committed to God's ways of doing and thinking, and he allowed God to guide his steps. At the end of his life, he held 299 patents. He believed in giving and tithing and, over time, he and his wife were giving 90% of their personal income to Kingdom purposes and living on the 10%. He said the question to ask was not how much of his money was to be given to God, but how much of God's money was to be kept for himself.

The idea of giving 90% of my income and living on the 10% was compelling to me. It was something I knew I wanted to do eventually in my life and, even though I was young, God had put another seed in my heart, another dream to go after. As I walked through the highs and lows of building my history with God, I found that He delights in redeeming our shortcomings and empowering the most unlikely individuals to accomplish exceedingly more than they can imagine, encouraging them to fulfill their God-given calling, and in doing so, bringing Him glory. I held this dream in my heart. It is still with me.

RECOGNIZING WEALTH

In junior high, my older sister and I attended a junior/senior high school about thirty minutes away from our home. As it was the only school in the mountains, all the kids from the whole area attended. The mountains had middle class folks and lower middle-class folks, like our family, and it also had very high-end families because of Big Bear Lake and Lake Arrowhead where many celebrities had vacation homes. This is where I began to notice the clothes other kids wore, the designer outfits and the perfect haircuts. I remember self-conscious feelings of that awkward age, and in any social situation, I would shrink and become as small as I possibly could so as to be unnoticeable.

One day in science class, I was leaning back in my chair as all the kids did from time to time. It was obviously taboo, but I was relaxed and not thinking when suddenly the chair slipped out from under me and I was lying on the floor staring at the ceiling while peals of laughter rang out all around. The science teacher's voice boomed out, "Sautter! Five hundred lines—'I will not lean back in my chair!'" Seriously, I felt like dying. My whole purpose for existence up to this point was to try to be invisible, not noticed, not known. Yet here I was, on the floor, the brunt of everyone's jokes that day. Yep, junior high life was tough.

During this time, my mom and sister cleaned a large fifteen bed-room, fourteen bathroom house in a gated community in the Lake Arrowhead area. We called it "The Castle." From what I remember, it was owned by some wealthy individual and used for conferences. From time to time, I went with my mom and sister and was always amazed at that place. It was a continuing education in understanding the different levels of society and where we fit into the mix.

MY MOM AND ME

Several significant things happened around my birth that my mom shared with me many times. I believe God's hand was on me in these special encounter moments so that over the years I wouldn't become too discouraged and give up on life. The first was when my mom was pregnant with me. She was in a store and saw a little girl with long, beautiful, thick hair whose name was Rebecca. My mom had a prophetic moment and said, "THIS baby's name will be Rebecca." God knew me before I was born. He fashioned me and formed me in my mother's womb. He had designs, plans and purposes for me and has had His hand on me my whole life, moving me down the timeline of His purpose.

I am Rebecca. The meaning of my name is that I am bound to the Lord, as Rebekah in scripture was bound to Isaac and meant to marry him. In the Old Testament, the names of people were very often attached to their assignments. There are incredible assignments and destinies hidden within the scripture. Many Bible people actually walked out the very definition of their names. Their names were enlightening to their behavior. In the same way, my name, Rebecca, has been a source of hope throughout my life, encouraging me that I am connected to my Lord's heart and I always have been. I have always known that. I have always felt the tug of His presence.

The second thing that brought me continual hope was my actual birth. I was born in the car with a police escort on the way to the hospital in the late-night hours. My dad drove as fast as he could as my mom was in labor in the back seat with my grandma helping her. A motorcycle cop stopped my dad for speeding and, when he heard what was happening, he escorted us to the hospital. I wasn't born just anywhere! I was born on Colorado Boulevard in Pasadena, California, the route of the Rose Parade! I always loved this being part of my story. It was another sign to me that God thought I was special and had a plan for my life.

That was a good thing. These two events in the story of my life were what I rehearsed over and over when I saw no good in myself. My mom often shared with me that when I was a two-year-old, I had rejected her, so she rejected me. She had tried to kiss me and I had turned my face away. That was enough for her to decide I was a difficult child and not worthy of her unconditional love. From that time on, I heard hundreds of times from my mom that I was defiant, rebellious, a jack-ass, bull-headed, disobedient and unmanageable. Those types of words were spoken over me again and again until I really believed that I was a very bad person with no redeemable qualities. I rarely opened up and talked, and never shared my thoughts or feelings with anyone, including the people in my family. In fact, I don't even know that I was aware that I had thoughts and feelings separate from what I was told about myself. I lived life in a dark place, trying to hide from people. I didn't like or trust people much at all. I just got through.

TWO BOOKS

There were two books that somehow came across my path in my early teen years. The first one was the book *None of These Diseases* by S.I. McMillen and David E. Stern. It showed how to obtain extraordinary medical benefits and live in divine health simply by heeding the Word of God. It helped me to believe God's guidelines for continual health and wholeness in my life. I determined to live by this–to accept and believe that God wanted me to live in divine health and that there was a way to do that.

Written in 1950, five years before I was born, *Visions Beyond the Veil* was another impacting book I read in my early teens. It opened my heart and spirit to the realities of the spiritual world. I was already experiencing some of these realities, but I just didn't know what they were. This book gave me a vision and even guidance as I walked in a realm no one was talking about in my Christian world. It was written by H.A. Baker, who, with his wife and co-worker, Josephine, began the Adullam Rescue Mission for street children in Yunnan Province, China.

The children in the home, mostly boys, ranged in age from six to eighteen. They began to have many spiritual experiences such as seeing heaven and even hell through a series of visions. The boys spent days in powerful meetings, praying and praising God. Under the anointing of the Holy Spirit, they prophesied, saw visions, and discovered how angels operated and protected people. God showed them unbelievers and what was to come for them in eternity. The hearts of the boys changed to be like the Father's heart and they began crying out to their neighbors to receive Jesus. I was transfixed. I wanted this in my life so badly. I wanted to bring these kinds of encounters to those I met. I wanted them for myself. I dreamed of the day when I would be leading a group of children and we would encounter God in this Heavenly way. I saw that this mighty outpouring was a fulfillment of God's promise, *"And it shall come to pass in the last days, saith God, I will pour out of My Spirit upon all flesh: and your sons and your daughters shall prophesy, and your young men shall see visions, and your old men shall dream dreams"* (Acts 2:17 KJV). Reading this book opened a door in my heart that has never been closed. It is a dream of my heart, even now, to see heaven come to earth this way and never stop.

NEW MEXICO

When I was thirteen, we moved to New Mexico where my parents joined United Indian Mission (UIM). My dad also taught school and drove a school bus first in Zuni, then in Gallup, thirty minutes away from where we lived in a small trading post area called Vanderwagen. We lived on a summer camp for Indian kids from all the different tribes in the region. Here, I could be wild and free. I could escape my dark thoughts when I was with the horses. I had nineteen horses and ponies to choose from, and I rode and cared for them daily. In the summers, I was a wrangler and took camp kids on rides. It was the very best place for me as I was emotionally scarred from my mom's continual negative assessments and verbal assaults. The horses were my safe place. They were peaceful. They accepted me. I remember telling God that I hated people but I loved the horses.

Once moving to New Mexico, it became clear to me that my mom had a poverty mentality and didn't like people who had wealth such as doctors or lawyers. She seemed to be intimidated by rich folk and made it a constant theme of lack that we didn't have what "they" had. Yet she loved Arabian horses and always talked about them. It was her strongest desire to have her own Arabian, but they can be very expensive, so it was a dream unfulfilled for her. In New Mexico, there was a doctor who boarded his horses at the camp. The doctor had some beautiful Morgan horses, and even that made mom angry. She felt nothing but distain for this doctor and his family, and we heard about it quite often. It was odd how something as simple as the type of horse someone preferred could set her off.

There was a lot of conflict over money between my mom and dad. Dad worked really hard, but it was never enough for mom. We all carried that poverty mentality into everything we did and had. We had "mission barrel" clothes–monthly we would get a big bag or box of others' cast-off clothing from churches in California our parents were associated with. We would sort through to find what fit us. Needless to say, we never looked trendy in our clothing styles! Sometimes, there would be food in the box. Once, there was a half-used box of cake mix. I remember being so angry that someone would think it was okay to gift something like that. I began to feel shame over who I was and what I had or didn't have during this time–that I wasn't good enough for nice things, for the best. I wasn't valuable. I believed this lie because it was what my family believed.

Economically, our family fit in well in New Mexico. It was a more level playing field as far as wealth distribution went. In fact, because we lived twenty miles out of the city of Gallup where our schools were, we had a long hour-and-a-half bus ride daily, picking up the Navajo kids along the route from their compounds. Their homes were often simple five- or six-sided "hogans" shaped like beehives and made of logs and mud. Their "yards" were just huge dirt areas out among the sagebrush and red rocks–never any grass, maybe a broken-down log fence surrounding a pitiful corn and bean patch. The homes had no wells and no running water.

Our camp had one well with a hose at the well house where Navajo families would come weekly for water. In the backs of their pick-up trucks, they carried fifty-five-gallon barrels to fill with water for their households. They presented themselves as very poor, but were far more well off than we were. Their value systems were just different. Many Navajo families had an abundance because of the turquoise and silver jewelry trade that went on in the area. They all made and sold their jewelry to the many traders in the area. Many families looked like they were in pitiful living situations, but also many had brand new pick-up trucks–Fords, Chevrolets, Dodges–which they had paid cash for. Such a different world we had been thrown into! But I loved it and didn't mind the crunch of lack.

Our first summer at the camp, we had to use the outhouse clear across the property since our septic tank hadn't been dug yet. In the early morning you would see us on our bikes hightailing it to that outhouse. It was embarrassing for a teenager, but we had no other choice! We had an old wringer washer for washing our clothes. In the summers, we could only wash our hair once a week because, with only one well, the camp would regularly run out of water. It was difficult showering only once a week since I was a wrangler and most summers were hot and dry, and the work was dirty and sweaty.

But, oh, how I loved, loved, loved it! I spent so much time with the horses and ponies, riding, taking others on rides, being outside and wild. As I got older, I graduated to other staff positions at the camp and finally to counselor the summer I was seventeen. I must have presented as a mature young lady, but I felt like an emotionally insecure train wreck on the inside.

SUPERNATURALLY AWARE

As a thirteen-year-old in New Mexico, I had a huge spiritual awakening. New Mexico's nickname is "Land of Enchantment" and I certainly began experiencing that enchantment in the negative spiritual arena. Our land and the land the camp was on was considered checkerboard land. This refers to land or acreage in certain western states that is organized in a checkerboard pattern. This acreage encompasses vast areas that are equal parts privately-owned property and federally-owned property. The areas are divided into sections, and each section is one square mile or 640 acres. Then the sections alternate in ownership between private individuals and the federal government. Our property was in a checkerboard area which bordered Navajo lands. We used the same roads, went to school on the same bus, and generally lived side-by-side with the Navajo people who were organized into family clans.

I began to encounter the demonic through the medicine men's (native sacred healers/spiritual leaders of the clans) ceremonies called "sings". These were family clan ceremonies to call for physical and mental healing for tribe members. These were done through sand paintings, chants, and dances, and were designed to "restore equilibrium to the cosmos." The sick person would be brought to a medicine man, simple outdoor "booths" were constructed with tree branches and log poles, and the clan's people would gather for up to nine days. The dogs around would howl and the demonic feeling was almost overwhelming, especially at night.

Fortunately, my mother had told us to use the Name of Jesus and speak the blood of Jesus whenever the "sings" took place. In the early hours of the morning, there were times I would "feel" and "see" a skeleton-like hand gripping my neck. I would wake up terrified and try to cry out, "Jesus!" Many times I could not even get my voice to work and I would feel paralyzed lying there in my bed. But even the *thought* of His name broke the evil power and I would be released.

Unfortunately, neither my church denomination, nor my Christian parents, ever addressed this spiritual battle that I had been flung into. My relationship and dependence on Jesus deepened during these years because He was my only hope and protection from living in this world of spiritual evil terror that I felt and "saw" so clearly. I began to build my life of faith by learning through experience. Like Abraham, I began to build my own history with God.

I came to realize I was highly sensitive, even in the physical realm. I knew things ahead of time. I could tell when something was wrong and just knew how to fix it. One of the ways this showed up was in my ability to work with horses. I could communicate quite well with them, they trusted me, and I trained many throughout my teens and early twenties. Many people commented on my intuitiveness and ability with horses. I had a knack, a seemingly special ability that was difficult to describe, but it was evident.

This also translated into food. I could tell the milk in the fridge was going sour three to four days before anyone in the rest of my family. This caused so much angst for my mother as I simply could not drink milk when I tasted and smelled it going bad. As I look back on these characteristics, I have come to realize that I was a "discerner" or "feeler" who was massively spiritually and naturally sensitive. It was showing up in every area of my life. Learning to manage it, trust what I was experiencing, and not believe I was the crazy one was the difficult part. I had to learn to ask what was going on in my heart when I felt something, acknowledge the fact that it was spiritual sensitivity, and that it was a benefit and a tool. I had to learn to rise above it, see it for what it really was, and call on the Holy Spirit for His discernment and help.

I also knew things concerning people. One of the big things was how my mom spoke. Even though by this time I had bought into the lie that I was a dark and terrible person because of her words over me, I hated how she talked to my dad and how she spoke about herself. She would constantly talk about how her mind was going, how she didn't have a good mind, how my dad was much smarter than she was, and that she couldn't think. She said many times that she must be losing her mind. She spoke negative things over and over about her mind, and I would cringe every time I heard her because I just knew that she shouldn't be speaking that stuff over herself. I knew there would be consequences.

Later, as I learned how to put my faith together with God's Word, I realized how many times God spoke about the power of the tongue, how it contains life and death (Proverbs 18:21), and that the tongue runs the whole life of a person (James 3). I began to study these verses and others that show how important what we say to ourselves, of ourselves, and to others is. I began to be more aware of what I was saying and, as I came out of my "silent" years, I tried to be strategic in my own speech.

BLUE MILK AND MARGARINE

A sure sign of our living with lack was something I didn't realize until I moved out of my parents' home. It was the blue milk. Because we were so limited financially, mom would buy powdered milk and mix it with whole milk so it would stretch further. While it was very wise to live within our means, I hated that light blue, almost transparent, milk. It was so thin and nasty tasting that I wouldn't drink it. Another trick mom used was replacing butter with margarine. Margarine was cheaper, but also not my favorite. When I left home, I never turned back to margarine again. It was so nice to be able to make those choices on my own.

Throughout our school years, we rarely, if ever, got to have a hot school lunch. It was just too expensive. So we brought our lunches from home. Mom made our lunches every day and they were good, healthy lunches, but it seemed that was just another way we stood out as being different and having less than everyone else. I was very aware what we could and couldn't afford and where we were placed on the wealth spectrum alongside my friends. We had our needs met, but rarely had our "wants" met. It was tough to navigate, but not destructive. We didn't have much, but we certainly didn't live in poverty. Our family just had a poverty mindset. This was something I needed to realize before I could take steps to break it over my life.

In high school, my friend Kathy also brought her own lunches from home. But Kathy had white bread for her sandwiches, store-bought lunchmeat, pop, and cookies. It was my dream to be able to eat that kind of food! Kathy, on the other hand, would look at my lunches with my mom's fried egg sandwiches made with homemade whole wheat bread, homemade cookies, healthy fruits and vegetables and wish she had that for lunch! Kathy and I worked a trade and all through high school we would split our lunches with each other so each of us could have a bit of what the other had.

This period of my life is when I really realized the disparity between the "haves" and the "have nots" and recognized that, in most ways, I was a "have not." One big source of this realization happened twice a year when the Navajo kids we rode the bus with received huge grocery bags full of new clothes–socks, shoes, tops, pants, jackets, underclothes, and more–through a government assistance program. I remember looking at those bags of brand new, beautiful clothes and longing for that for me. One time I asked my Navajo friend Stacia what she was going to do with all those great clothes and she said, "I don't need them. I will just throw them out into the sage brush on my walk home." I was devastated. I so wanted to tell her to give them to me! It broke my heart.

Of course, at that time, I didn't realize that my dad, through his hard work, paid taxes that were then partially used to buy these things. I didn't know the history of the Navajo people with the U.S. Government and all the political dealings behind the scenes that caused these kinds of hand-outs to take place. I certainly didn't realize that the government is us, that nothing is free, that someone, somewhere has to pay for it. But as I got educated in finances and understood better how government and politics work, I gained some understanding. Still, it grieves my heart to think of how many bags of clothes were despised and thrown into the sage brush through those years ... and how many little Caucasian missionary kids like me could have put those clothes to good use.

GOD'S PLANS AND PURPOSES

The summer of my seventeenth year, I became a counselor at our camp. A young girl named Lisa was placed in my cabin. I have remembered her forever because she was nine or so years old and had a brain tumor. She was going blind in one eye. One side of her body was beginning to be paralyzed because of the tumor. Lisa was going through radiation and wasn't expected to live very long. They thought the tumor was the result of a horse-riding accident she had had a year before. I was a young teen and a bit freaked out that she was in my cabin, hoping nothing went wrong medically with her while in my care. But she was a bubbly, happy, sweet girl, and it was a good week. Her parents had come to pastor our church in Gallup but didn't stay beyond that year. They moved on. I often thought of Lisa through the years and wondered whatever happened to her.

Watching the hand of God on my life and seeing His plans and purposes play out as He has kept me in the palm of His hand is one of the most amazing things to me as I look back through my life. In the case of Lisa, it went like this:

In June of 2013, thirty-nine years after the summer I was a seventeen-year-old counselor at Summer Park Ranch, I attended a worship school at Bethel Church in Northern California. My kids and I rented a room in a house with a few gals from all over the U.S. who were attending the worship school, as well. As I visited with one of the ladies, I learned she was Lisa's sister, the same Lisa I had been a counselor to thirty-nine years before! She told me that Lisa had lived a long and happy life with her family (with a fifteen-year-old mentality) and passed away at age forty-nine just that spring. My housemate, Judy, Lisa's sister, was only a six-month-old baby when Lisa was in my cabin all those years ago. Since the family had moved away shortly after that summer, I had never met this sister.

Judy quickly emailed her mom to tell her about this amazing co-incidence and her mom, remembering me and my family in New Mexico, said, "*Wow! Is this Becky Sautter (my maiden name)? Lisa mentioned her often with such fond memories right up till she died. This Godcidental brought tears to my eyes. God is so very, very good.*"

When I heard that email message on the morning of June 26, 2013, it brought tears to MY eyes that God had orchestrated all this, that now I finally knew, thirty-nine years later, what happened to Lisa. Crazy that God would put both her younger sister and me in the same house for two weeks that summer! He was really showing me how much impact we have on others throughout our whole lives, and most of the time we don't even know it. How very significant each and every relationship is!

I was told that, over the years, Lisa would mention me and ask her family, "Do you remember Becky?" Of course, her sister didn't as she was only a baby back then, and she would get so frustrated with Lisa because Lisa would direct the family in praying for me and my family during their prayer times. Wow! I feel so grateful and humbled, because when I was seventeen, I felt like a nobody with nothing to give, unimportant, and extremely insignificant. But I had a dream that God would use me someday. It was so amazing that He was already using me in the life of this little girl and I didn't even know it!

It took years of walking it out with Jesus to come to know my identity in Him. I believe that, over the years as Lisa remembered me, she lifted a lot of prayer to the Father on my behalf. Now she is in heaven dancing with Jesus, all healed and whole. I am so happy, so in awe of Him and His amazing ways. God is very, very good!

Understanding my identity and who I am in Christ, how loved I am by God, has been a giant key in the financial journey I have been on. Giving and giving and giving some more has been the main thing that started getting my view of myself into alignment, but it was just one part of it. I was learning to hear His voice as I stepped out and gave. I was learning to hear God and obey. I was learning to notice the people He was noticing, those He wanted me to notice. When I heard Him say something, I would step out and pursue it and do it as quickly as possible. I was gaining confidence that He would take care of me, always guide me, and never leave me alone.

Again, the hand of God has been on me throughout and His guidance is impeccable. Truly to Him, the journey and maturity process in my life was by far more valuable than the final destination. What He seems to delight in is the process, the journey, rather than the ending. My process has been messy most of my life, but I believe His pleasure has rested on me because I have kept on going. Instead of believing and speaking the negative, I choose to believe and speak that I am tenacious, staunch, unswerving, determined, and steadfast. When I lock onto something, like a pit bull, I don't let go until I see the results. I think that character trait along with relentless, radical giving has been the biggest key to where I am now.

Chapter 2

ON THE ROAD TO MATURITY

I definitely realized the financial stress my family was under when I was in high school and began my first job. I worked in Gallup and drove the twenty miles back and forth on Highway 32 regularly. My dad had always meticulously kept records of mileage whenever we got gas, and he required that of us as well. Each vehicle had a little book where we would write the date, the mileage, the gallons of gas bought and the cost. Then we would subtract the mileage from the last written amount, divide by the gallons bought and we would then know how many miles per gallon we were getting in the car. We had two vehicles; one a family carry-all and another small gas saver car–never new, always on the verge of breaking down. I lived in fear of a potential breakdown and being stranded at night on that highway! One night I had a dream where I had somehow found out that if I drove in reverse the whole way home, the car wouldn't use any gas at all. That was when I realized how worried I was about money and also how much I wanted to please my dad and make him proud of me for figuring out a way to save money for our family.

But it was also during these years that I caught the fire of relationship with God and never looked back. When I was nineteen, I was driving home on Highway 32 one night after work, telling God that up to this point in my life He had been my parents' God, and that if He was real and was to be my God, He needed to show me. I was pretty raw, honest and straightforward with Him.

Within a month, Jon and Mindy, a young married couple, came to the Ranch to be the staff leaders for the summer. They brought the concept of a living God to me, a God who was concerned about ME, a God who wanted relationship with ME. They spoke of us being tripartite beings made up of spirit, soul and body and introduced me to Watchman Nee's book, *The Normal Christian Life*. I had been raised in evangelical churches all my life, but I had never had this explained so clearly. I completely lit up on the inside. I was sold out and hungry for God from that time on. It was like my mind was awakened to my spirit and I became constantly aware of God and His thoughts within me. I was beginning to learn His ways and processes.

YOUNG ADULT STRUGGLES

After high school, I went to college in Los Angeles. My parents had a requirement that each of us must attend at least one year of a Bible college before going on to another college of our choice, but they didn't have any savings to help us get through college. At this point, money really became an issue because I literally didn't have any. I did get a few scholarships and grants to go to BIOLA, but I also had to take out a loan. This was greatly distressing to me, since I had not been given much wisdom in money matters. In college, I just lived month-to-month, never even having enough money to telephone and touch base with my parents consistently. During one period, three months went by before I heard from them—there were no cell phones at this time, so connecting needed to be via land lines. We could not call out from our dorms, so I had to use a pay phone to call my parents. Meanwhile, I worked in the college coffee shop and used all of that money for tuition, room, board, and living expenses.

While at BIOLA, I was such a lonely soul. I felt completely out of place in the city, surrounded by students who had been raised in worlds so different from mine. My life in the rural wilds of New Mexico, surrounded by sagebrush, ancient Anasazi ruins, daily riding horses through the dry arroyos, and picking piñons to sell at the trading post was so different from the cultured city life I was now struggling to be a part of.

I transferred in as a sophomore, so I was not put into the normal freshman dorm, but was put in Zeta Chi, a duplex that housed five upperclassman girls. There was me with my little twin bed and desk in a corner and four girls, all of them seniors. They had known one another throughout their years at BIOLA and enjoyed connection and relationship with each other, which left me as the odd one out. They were very sweet and kind, but were on such a different trajectory in life than I was.

Each of them had a huge three-ring binder for wedding planning, something all of them were into. They were determined to not leave BIOLA without a husband. They had different sections for the wedding dresses, the cakes, the announcements, the rings, and much more. These binders were filled with their hopes and dreams for their weddings. Only two of the girls even had boyfriends! BIOLA even had nicknames for this mindset–girls were BIOLA Bettys and guys were BIOLA Bobs. This whole way of thinking was really shocking to me and I couldn't relate, so I kept to myself, went to classes, went to work at the coffee shop, and tried to manage life in college the best I could.

GOD'S PROVISION

Fortunately, God had His hand on me and had given me a wonderful New Mexico connection through Jon and Mindy from the camp the previous summer. Mindy's sister, Candie, and her husband Todd, were in California and lived close to BIOLA. They would pick me up from time to time, feed me dinner, and take me to church, nurturing and caring for me as if I were a little sister. Todd worked at NBC, and many times Candie and I would go to the NBC studios to watch a show being taped and then go out for a fancy dinner after. They loved me so well and showed me a more cultured life than my backwoods upbringing at the camp in New Mexico.

There was a small chapel on the campus which became my safe place. I missed my family, my horses, and my free-spirited life so much. One of my great reliefs from the pain in my heart was to go daily to the chapel, get on my knees and cry out to God. I so wanted to hear His voice, to feel His presence, to know Him. I was such a naïve young country girl, and I needed God to hold my heart. I needed to hold His hand and be held by Him.

In my last year at BIOLA, Candie's younger sister, Julie, began attending the college and, even though by then I was in off-campus housing and she was on campus, we hung out and had a great friendship. She and I even shared the same birthday! I was treated as a part of their family. God was showing His love and care for me through these amazing friends.

One Easter break when I wasn't able to go back home to New Mexico, this family invited me to spend the week with them in Los Gatos, California. While there, Julie and I both worked for the week in a small, local amusement park. I worked at the concession stand making cotton candy and serving up fair food. Easter morning arrived and I was blown away because, along with Julie, I received an abundant Easter "basket" from Julie's mom. It was a yellow Tupperware mixing bowl filled with green Easter grass, wooden spoons, spatulas, and all kinds of chocolate eggs and bunnies. I had never received an Easter gift in my life, and I was absolutely floored. I kept that bowl for years, until the bottom fell off and it was completely worn out. It was one of the best gifts ever and just another way God showed me His love by singling me out and letting me know I was special.

The first time I ever flew in an airplane was to San Francisco from Los Angeles to be with this same family for Thanksgiving. Todd and Candie took me out to dinner at the Hyatt Regency Hotel in San Francisco. I had never been in such a place and really felt like a country bumpkin as my mouth fell open at every turn seeing the amazing architecture of that four-star hotel, all the lavish richness and luxury. I was completely out of my element! Later, we drove up to Grants Pass, Oregon to spend Thanksgiving with Jon and Mindy in their cool log house. Again, I was welcomed into the family as one of their own.

These girls were actually the granddaughters of famous movie and television personalities Roy Rogers and Dale Evans. Their father was Dale's son, so I got to hang out with Roy and Dale from time to time, as well. Julie and I would go to Calvary Chapel Costa Mesa with Grandma Dale when she was in town. She would sing at the top of her lungs, so full of confidence, that Julie and I would cringe with embarrassment!

I was also privileged to attend Julie's college graduation from BIOLA with Roy, Dale and the rest of the family in the college's Presidential Office overlooking the ceremonies. During that time, I didn't realize what an honor it was to be connected with this family, but looking back, I can see God watching out for me–a young, struggling, unsure soul. Sadly, I was so young, I didn't realize what a great gift God had given me in this family. They were loving, caring and so giving, wanting to take me in, love me, lavish me with gifts, and include me. What a gift that I have tried to give to others many times over the years since.

DEBT

One of my lessons at BIOLA was how different I was from so many of the students whose families were wealthier than mine. BIOLA was a private college, one of the three largest Christian colleges in the country, so it was attractive and affordable to a wealthier clientele. Many of my classmates had a free pass. They didn't have to work to make their way through college. They had nice looking cars. They were free to come and go and spend money on clothes, dorm room décor, fancy food, and other things they wanted. I worked every day in the college coffee shop. I applied for grants. I took out a student loan. Even though my parents couldn't give finances toward my college education, I did have a healthy understanding of the value of a dollar because I had to pay my own way.

When I left BIOLA after three years, in 1977, I had $3,000 in student loan debt (today's value would be around $18,000). This was horrifying, and I was overwhelmed with the thought of owing money and having no job to pay it off. I also left BIOLA without a degree, but moved to Albuquerque, New Mexico to finish it at the University of New Mexico, which was much cheaper since I was a resident of New Mexico and it was a state college. My biggest regret at this time is that I just didn't know. Had I known that I could get just as good of an education by attending UNM, I would have only spent one year at BIOLA and finished my undergrad work in New Mexico. As it turned out, because I transferred colleges, I had to repeat one whole year of coursework. It was exactly the same courses I had taken at BIOLA, but the course names and descriptions were different, so they were not accepted. As a clueless nineteen-year-old, I just did what was considered "normal."

The feelings I had about being in that much debt bordered on sheer terror. I had no idea how I would pay it all off while still going to school. I had numerous part time jobs, lived with roommates, paid further tuition payments with cash and slowly but surely whittled the debt down. I don't even remember how long it took me to pay it all off–probably a number of years–but I finally did and was so greatly relieved to be completely out of debt. I never wanted to experience debt again in my life. The weight of it was very heavy. I saw again how true God's Word is when He says in Proverbs 22:7, "*The rich rule over the poor, and the borrower is slave to the lender*" (NIV).

That was one thing my parents did bless me with–the understanding that debt was a bad thing. I had no credit cards at all and didn't want any. I didn't have much money, but I was learning to hear His voice, although I was still struggling with my identity in Him and what He thought about me.

JESUS WAS THERE

During my twenties, I moved back and forth between Albuquerque, New Mexico and Los Angeles, California a couple times trying to find my bearings. In California, God placed me in a church that began to stir my soul with the message of faith. I had so much of the Word in my heart from my childhood, but I didn't have a relationship with God as a loving, providing Father. God began to mend this broken part of me in amazing ways.

One day I was reading a book that was all about inner healing. The author was talking about the heart of the Father God, and said to bring to mind a traumatizing time dealing with our own earthly father. I knew exactly what that time was.

Lying on the sunbathed floor in front of the large picture window in my apartment, I pictured myself as a ten-year-old girl standing in front of my father at his desk. My older and younger sisters and my cousin were there, as well. We were standing in a line and being asked about a banana peel my dad had found on the ground on our property. We had all been given bananas as a snack and were told to throw the peels in the trash when done. One of us hadn't done that. To this day, I do not know who had dropped the peel (it very well could have been me), but dad's questioning was intense and severe with punishment being given out that no one would "fess up." I remember sobbing uncontrollably as the interrogation continued seemingly forever.

Then I did as the author in the book suggested and asked Jesus where He was in that place. Suddenly I "saw" him as a twelve-year-old young man standing in our line-up, the first one in front of my dad. When Dad asked the question again, "Who did it?" Jesus answered, "I did." Then He took the punishment. And at the age of twenty-four, I was suddenly free of fear of my father. My heart was filled with empathy and compassion which, years later, manifested as I took care of him in the last ten years of his life up to his death at the age of ninety. It was such an honor to care well for him, and I am sure that Jesus walked me through that encounter years before, knowing that caring for my dad well would be part of my calling. I never could have done it if I had offense, fear, and anger in my heart toward him.

Through these years, I was learning to hear Him, to connect the Word inside me with the measure of faith that had been given (Romans 12:3). I began to see the verses I had learned as a child from a heavenly perspective. For instance, I knew quite well Hebrews 11:6 which says, "*But without faith it is impossible to please Him, for he that cometh to God must believe that He is,*" (KJV) but somehow, I stopped there. Suddenly the revelation came that there was more to that verse and it was for ME. I saw the part that says, "*and that He is a rewarder of those who diligently seek Him*" (KJV). I realized He wanted to reward ME. This was so huge for me. It set me free when I began realizing He wasn't mad at me, but He had great and enduring love for me. Such great love for me. I still had a long way to go, but He was in hot pursuit of me. I am so thankful.

As I look back, God always had me in the right place, at the right time. He was always guiding me by His counsel with His eye upon me (Psalm 32:8; Psalm 73:24). I was learning to walk by faith, not by sight. I was beginning to see His "super" on my "natural." Financially, I was doing okay, continuing to tithe as I had been taught throughout my life, but pretty much still living from paycheck to paycheck, month to month.

This is the period of time when I began to speak declarations of His Word over my life. As the Word opened up to me in faith, I came into an understanding of the power of the tongue and the importance of my own words, how they could and would change my life for the better or the worse, whichever I chose to speak. "*Life and death are in the power of the tongue. And those who love it will eat its fruit*" (Proverbs 18:21 NKJV). So I put my tenacity to work for me and began declaring who I was and what His Word said about me.

MY 3X5 CARDS

Another book came across my path at just the right time. In this book, the author suggested taking ten 3x5 cards and on each one writing something positive about oneself, then reading them out loud every day to begin changing the negative, hurtful lies and wounds that may have been lodged there. I got my ten cards but couldn't think of more than two things to write. I went ahead and wrote those two things: I have long, beautiful hair, and I make good chocolate chip cookies. Since those were the only two things I could think of that were good about me, I began saying those every day. Eventually, my card stack expanded as did my self-awareness and self-love.

After I spent some time on self-love and speaking good things over me to counteract all the negatives I had heard throughout my childhood, teen, and young adult years, I graduated on to speaking God's Word and His promises over my life.

As a young child, I was sure that God loved Israel so much more than me, and I wished I had been born a Jew to be in that special privileged group of people. Then, as with all the other parts of scripture that were opening up, Galatians 3:29 (NKJV) became alive to me: "*If you are Christ's, then you are Abraham's seed, and heirs according to the promise.*" Oh, how this thrilled my soul! I had no doubt that I was IN Christ, so now all those promises became mine. What a great understanding to have gained. My history with God moved a little further, a little deeper.

At one point, I was privileged to be at a conference in Southern California where Lester Sumrall and Norvel Hayes, great men of faith, were speaking. The miracles they walked in, their histories and connections with God, were all amazing. I was soaking up everything I heard. I was in the prayer line every time there was one offered and I received so much from God. But probably the greatest thing I received was listening to Norvel Hayes as he told stories of his life of faith.

He said something that hit me so hard, I still say it today forty years later: *I am NEVER confused!* I know, it seems so simple and it sounds simple when I say it, but after saying it thousands and thousands of times throughout the years, it has become such truth in my life. I am truly NEVER confused ... I ALWAYS hear His voice and know what to do, when to do it and where to go.

YOU SHOULD HAVE BEEN BORN A BOY

As a young girl, many times I didn't feel I was normal or that I fit. I sensed, probably wrongly, that my parents would have rather had a boy instead of me, the second-born girl. I was also considered a "tomboy" throughout my childhood and had people tell me several times that I should have been born a boy. The statements were made when I accomplished something they thought was amazing, something perhaps they didn't think a girl or young woman should be able to do.

One of the most hurtful times was when I was working with a high school youth group and the leader called me aside to tell me that I had so much ability, he didn't understand why I was a woman, that I should have been born a man. It was so confusing. I knew I had huge capacity. I loved to dream and accomplish, but so many people seemed to want to stop me, put me in a box, and keep me from expanding. I didn't understand why I had all this ability, all this passion, all this leadership capability, and yet I wasn't released to flow in it.

I loved Isaiah 54:1-6 where God told Israel to shout for joy, to break forth into joyful shouting, to enlarge the place of their tent, to stretch out, that they would spread abroad to the right and to the left. I put my faith to this passage and believed it was for me. But I didn't see how it was being walked out step-by-faltering-step in my life. Thus, I continued to believe the lie that I was not perfectly created to be what God wanted me to be. I would go to God constantly and ask, 'Why did You create me? Is there anything good about me?'

But I stayed steadfast to the Word of God, kept pouring it into me, kept clinging to His Heart as the journey of renewing my mind continued, although this gender issue was perhaps the hardest one as it was so deep-seated and went back to early in my life. It is still something I am working on to this day because my personality is a strong one, not the typical feminine version that many churches prefer. I have a strong voice, a quick mind, and an ability to see issues very clearly and thoroughly. I have solutions, but at the time, no one seemed to want to hear them, so I poured myself into the areas I felt confident in. These areas were horse training, my school teaching, and administrating children's ministries. But a strong spirit of rejection was taking hold in my life. I know I created an atmosphere of rejection around me, and I pretty much went into hiding when I felt resistance or conflict brewing. I just didn't want to hear the critical voice from others, especially when I was battling that critical voice on the inside of me as well.

HEARING HIS VOICE

Jesus said, *"My sheep hear My voice and I know them and they follow Me"* (John 10:27 KJV). I added that to my group of declarations: *I hear the voice of Jesus, my good shepherd, and the voice of another I will NEVER follow!* I also decided that if God's Word told me to do or say something, I would do it. In Proverbs, we are told to call Wisdom our sister, to call Understanding our intimate friend, and to cry out for Discernment. More declarations were added: *Wisdom, you are my sister; Understanding, you are my closest friend; I cry out for Discernment, in Jesus' Name.* I continued to add declaration after declaration to my list and I spoke them out regularly.

God wasn't interested in working with me on lack or prosperity or increase at this time. I believe because my identity was so fractured, I just needed to learn and experience His love for me. I needed to grow up in Him. So that's what we worked on. One of the greatest desires of my heart was to be married, but there seemed to be no one interested in marrying me. So instead of going out to bars, partying, trying to find a guy, and waiting for the phone to ring, I would go home after work every day and read chapter after chapter of the Word. I would read thirty to sixty chapters a night. I also would listen to teaching tapes over and over, so much so the cassette tape recording I kept beside my bed stayed running while I slept. If I woke up and it was finished on one side, I would flip it over and go back to sleep. I poured into my spirit the voices of those who were doing the works that Jesus did, those who were teaching, preaching, working miracles, and walking in great faith. It was a huge time of planting much seed, or as Marilyn Hickey put it, "canning" the harvest for the future winter that is coming.

I was pouring the Word in me during this waiting period. I also began to get a revelation of Psalm 37:4 (ESV) "*Delight yourself in the Lord and He will give you the desires of your heart.*" I began to get a deeper understanding as I mixed the Word of God in my heart with faith, that not only did God want to give me desires I knew I had, but He would also place desires in my heart that I didn't even know I wanted or needed. It was like a light bulb went off in my head and heart as I processed what that really meant for me. Slowly, I was beginning to experience the love of God for me in real time, learning to hear His voice more clearly.

SEEING DEMONS

The church I attended in Pasadena, California was opening up to the move of the Holy Spirit. I was learning the history of revivals throughout the earth and was hungry for more. We had a group of committed, passionate Christians going hard after God. One Sunday, the church secretary/receptionist was signing people up for a retreat weekend the church was hosting. I was standing beside her at the table she had set up outside the sanctuary. She and I were chatting away when I felt a hand on my shoulder. I turned, and there was a lady I had never seen before standing there. But suddenly, I wasn't looking into a lady's eyes, I was looking into a demon's eyes. It was terrifying, and I had no clue what to do. Not only did I see this demon looking out of her eyes at me, but I felt this electricity surge going back and forth between us. I couldn't pull my eyes away from her. I knew what this was because of my New Mexico upbringing and experiences with the supernatural.

Finally, I put my hand on her arm and was able to pry my eyes away. I later asked my friend if she had seen and felt what I did. She didn't, but she trusted that I had experienced something (probably because I was so freaked out) and suggested I go to one of the pastors and tell them what had happened. I did, but no one really knew what to do about it. They just said they would keep an eye out to see if anything happened during the service with this lady. Nothing did, and the moment passed without further incident. But I often wondered why that had happened to me, why I experienced the demonic so clearly. I would wonder and ask God but never received a definitive answer, so I figured the devil pretty much hated me so much, he wanted to taunt me whenever he could. I became pretty wary.

The next time something similar happened, I was mentoring a group of high school girls. I had piled five of them in my car, and we were going out for a Saturday afternoon of fun together. We had stopped at a grocery store to pick up some items and, as we were leaving, a homeless Navajo lady sitting along the side of the store called out to us. We went over. One of my gals, Shelly, was a super evangelist, so I was quite willing to let her talk to this lady. But the lady pinpointed me and fixed me with her gaze. Her eyes changed, and suddenly there was a demon staring out at me. This time, there was an electrical force pulsating back and forth between me and her. I was squatted down looking at the lady and I couldn't pry my eyes away, so I just shut them, put my hand on the lady's arm, and began to pray. When I opened my eyes, I was seeing the actual person again. I was so relieved! We bought the lady a sandwich, Shelly ministered to her, and we left. I asked the girls if they had seen what I had. Again, they said no, but Shelly had felt the electrical surges and knew something was happening in the spirit realm. She just didn't see it.

It was another puzzling moment, and I was left wondering why, what was the purpose of these demonic encounters? Was it just to intimidate me? Was I somehow dangerous to Satan's realm? I really didn't see how because I was just being a regular Christian, doing the best I could, working with youth groups, teaching school, and trying to figure out how to be a young adult. It didn't seem like I was doing any great damage to the demonic realm. Sadly, no church I knew of had any answers for me.

PRAY!

I was about twenty-six years old and was at the Rose Parade on New Year's Day in Pasadena, California. This parade is HUGE with massive floats and thousands of people—a very well-known and famous yearly parade. All the floats are covered completely in flower petals and they are gorgeous, colorful, and so very big.

I was there with friends, packed in with all the other people, watching the floats, horses, and bands come by. Suddenly, I heard the Holy Spirit say, "PRAY!" It was so strong that I immediately covered my mouth with my hand and started praying in the spirit quietly and fervently.

When I looked up, I saw a Mark Twain Steamboat float with huge twenty-foot-high smoke stacks slowly moving toward us down the street. There were beautifully dressed Southern men and women smiling and waving from the top deck. But there was a problem because the smoke stacks were too tall for the electrical power lines that crossed Colorado Boulevard, and the driver of the float couldn't see that. The beautiful people on the float didn't see the problem either, but the crowd on both sides of the street did. I knew why Holy Spirit had given me the urgent call to pray. I kept praying and the smoke stacks hit the power lines. They began stretching and stretching while the whole crowd stood riveted. Suddenly the power lines snapped. They were hot, live wires, and they were arcing electricity, spinning around in the air on both sides of the road like wild snakes. I kept praying, then just as suddenly, the power lines on both sides of the street dropped to the ground, quit moving and lay there. Miraculously, they didn't hit a person–either in the crowd on both sides of the street or anyone on the float–no one was hurt. That was one of the first times I "heard" His voice and I knew He had chosen me because I would hear and I would respond. It was a remarkable experience in hearing His voice, an experience I have never forgotten.

BEAUTIFUL EYES

God just kept adding more and more value to me during these years. One of the most significant times was in 1987. I was working on my Master's Degree from the University of New Mexico. I was in a small program with about thirteen of us studying Educational Administration. I had had a difficult fall on several levels.

I was teaching in a huge elementary school in Rio Rancho, New Mexico. Because of tremendous growth in the area, the school had almost twice the number of students enrolled than the buildings could hold. When I was hired as a first year fifth grade teacher, the administration told the four other fifth grade teachers to pick out two of their academically solid students who were on grade level in reading and math, and they would be moved to the new classroom. I also got fourteen students from the fourth/fifth combination class they were closing. The other teachers gave me the most challenging fifth graders in the whole school. All these kids had been in this school since kindergarten and they were dominators. I truly thought I was going crazy with all of their daily rebellion and issues. It was completely overwhelming to a new teacher.

My one consolation was my friend, the music teacher, Ron. He helped keep me sane as I navigated the daily difficulties of this class. Ron knew these kids and realized very quickly that the other teachers gave me their most difficult problem students. He had empathy for me, but I struggled.

I struggled on multiple other levels, as well. Financially, I was barely making it month to month. I wasn't saving any money at all for the future—that wasn't even on my grid. I had bought a new car on payments (something I would later learn to never do again!) and my relationship with my mother was still pretty bad.

I went home to Vanderwagen, New Mexico for Christmas break to meet with my parents and two of my siblings. We were going to drive to Tucson to spend Christmas with my other sister, her husband and young son. I was thirty-two years old at the time.

When I got home, the usual playbook began to run with my mom ordering me to do certain chores: iron her scarf, cut and package the fudge, wash the dishes, vacuum the house, put the dog leashes, collars and food in the truck, clean the kitchen, and more. Meanwhile my twenty-four-year-old brother was just messing around in his room, and my twenty-eight-year-old sister was sitting on the couch reading *Vogue*. I had been working to please my mom from the moment I had arrived. At one point, she confronted me about where I had put the dog leashes. I told her I had put them in the truck, but when I realized I had not put them in the place she wanted, I got defensive, and my voice and body language reflected that. She became very angry and told me, "*Don't speak to me in that tone of voice! You are defiant, rebellious, belligerent, a jack-ass, and bull-headed. You just try and deny it!*"

She had never told me to try and deny all those things before. In less than a split-second, the thought came through my mind, *If I am the righteousness of God in Christ Jesus, I can't be those things she says I am. I may act those ways sometimes, but that is not who I am.*

So, feeling like chopped liver inside, I said, "*I deny it.*"

Instantly, her face contorted in the most intense anger I had ever seen, and she erupted with angry and terrifying words. Again, I felt like I was looking into the eyes of a demon, but that didn't seem possible as I knew my mom was a believer, in spite of her constant intense anger toward all of us. My dad was standing there trying to make peace. It was such a horrible situation. Somehow it ended, and we did drive down to Tucson–which also ended poorly. In those moments, I decided to never allow my mother to call me names again. I was finished.

When I got back home to Albuquerque, I began teaching again and resumed my graduate classes. Within two weeks in January, three people told me I had beautiful eyes. I had never had this happen before. Many times people had commented on my long and thick hair, but never my eyes. The third person was Clarence, an older guy in my grad class. He said, "Becky, has anyone ever told you that you have beautiful eyes?" I was astounded.

I told him yes, that he was the third person in two weeks. The first one was the attendant at a gas station as I was pumping gas. He just flat out told me, "You have beautiful eyes!" The second was my pastor who I was close to as I babysat his kids often. My car was parked at the university, and when I went out after my class there was a little post-it note on the window that said, "Hey, Beautiful eyes!" with a little hand-drawn picture of eyes. And then a couple days later, Clarence asked me the question. When I told him about these other two incidents, he said, "*You are probably looking people in the eye now and you weren't before. You are growing up, Becky. You are growing up!*"

In all this, I realized that something had been broken over me when I had denied the accusations of my mother. And even though I had to work hard to move forward, to really believe what God said about me to counter all those years of believing the negative, I was on the journey and I gave it my all.

ADDING MORE VALUE

As I mentioned, I was close with my pastor and his family. I would watch their two kids when they went on speaking trips and such. One of those times I showed up and there was a silver Porsche 928 in the driveway. I was amazed. It was used but a very nice car. It was just beautiful. As my pastors were packing up, he threw me the keys and said, "*Go ahead and use it while we are gone!*"

I was stunned. Of course, I did use it! I found I needed to go to the grocery store several times, so I packed the kids up and off we went. What this did to my heart was to open me up to my value. It broke some old lies that I was not deserving of nice things, that I would never have more than 'just enough.' I am so grateful to my pastor for seeing the value in me and affirming it by letting me drive that car. It also opened me up to the possibility that someday I could have nice things—maybe not a Porsche 928, but new things, new clothes, new shoes, new furniture … that maybe, just maybe, I was worth it.

IT IS COMING - WAIT FOR IT

It was during this time that I was involved in the children's ministry of my church. One spring the children's pastor, Sheri, chose a team of volunteers to travel from Albuquerque to Tulsa, Oklahoma to attend a week-long children's ministry training at a really cool camp for kids. I was on the team, and it was a great week. We were out at the camp in the old west town setting, doing all the things the camp kids would do—canoeing, horseback riding, bumper cars, swimming, and experiencing it all. In the mornings and evenings, we would have training meetings. It was Thursday evening, and we had one more day before camp was over and we would return to New Mexico. There were about fifty people attending this training from all over the world. The speaker finished up and then had all of us stand in a big circle in the room. I was exhausted and just wanted to go back to my bunk bed and crash. But I stayed and stood. The camp director then told us to listen to the Holy Spirit, and when He highlighted someone, we were to go to that person to speak a word of encouragement or whatever He had spoken. I stood there feeling and sensing nothing.

The whole week I had been crying out to God for what I wanted most in the whole world, a husband, ministry, and family of my own. I had come to the understanding that as I delighted myself in the Lord, He would give me the desires of my heart—not only would He fulfill the desires, but He would place the desires in my heart that He wanted me to have. I was very confident by this age that it was

God's blessing for me to marry someday. I was thirty-two. I had had people come to me over the years questioning me about why I wasn't married, encouraging me to go to bars to find a husband as there are good guys there, asking what was wrong with me, etc. I was pretty much done with that, but I kept going to God and asking Him for the answers.

So, there I stood that night at camp, feeling nothing. Then the camp director came up to me and said, "The Lord wants me to pray with you about the desires of your heart." Instantly, I felt a pillar-like column of electricity rushing through me from the top of me to the floor, and I knew God was there. I said, "Okay."

He said, "What is the desire of your heart?" My heart sank as I realized I had to verbalize it, and I felt it would sound so petty, selfish, and foolish. But I tentatively said anyway, "To have a husband." Instantly, I felt like I had blown it because in reality I didn't just want a husband, I wanted a life partner to do ministry together with, to soar, to fly, to reach for the heavens together and see God's Kingdom come. But I didn't get any of that out.

The Holy Spirit must have interpreted for me to the director because he said,

"That's right, and God wants you to know three things -

Number one, wait for it, it is coming.

Number two, it will be glorious above all you ask or think; and

Number three, the two of you will bring many souls into the Kingdom."

And I cried. This was it! God knew. This was everything I was hoping and dreaming for. God knew me! He wanted the same things for me that I wanted for myself! But instantly, I also realized that when God tells you to wait for something, it could be years and years. If He was telling me to wait, then there WOULD be a wait. I knew about Abraham and Sarah and their twenty-five-year wait. I knew about Joseph and his thirteen-year wait. I knew about Paul and his thirteen to fourteen-year wait in the desert before setting out in ministry for Jesus. Another period of more waiting loomed ahead. At least this time, the waiting would be easier because I had a promise from God, a dramatic promise given in a dramatic way!

FINDING LOST THINGS

At this time, I was teaching in Albuquerque, attending a great church, and continuing to have my mind renewed to who I really was in Christ with all He wanted for me. Because I realized I had a lot of negativity to overcome, I decided to begin to live a lifestyle of giving. I knew that even though I didn't have much, God would meet me with my little bit of faith. One service, we were singing the chorus, *"Lord, You are more precious than silver. Lord, You are more costly than gold. Lord, You are more beautiful than diamonds and nothing I desire compares with You."* (Deshazo 1982) As we sang, I heard the Lord very clearly ask me, *'Is what you are saying really true? Do you really believe I am more valuable to you than money and things?'* Instantly, I was gently convicted. I fell to my knees in my heart and vowed to put Him first, even if I had nothing. He would always be more precious to me than anything else.

My church started a program called, *"Could You Not Tarry One Hour,"* going through Pastor Larry Lea's Prayer Guide of the Lord's prayer. Our church opened at six a.m. every morning for people who might want to pray for an hour before work. I began going, seeking God with all my heart. I also began giving one dollar a week in my church's offering. I was learning how to link my faith with my gift. I knew that the angel had said to Cornelius in Acts 10 that his prayers and alms had risen as a memorial before God. I wanted to be like that. I wanted wholeness in my brokenness. I wanted to be completely healed and whole from all the junk and lies I believed about myself. So I began a journey of giving, not for financial gain, although that would have been appreciated, but for emotional and mental healing to find out who I was meant to be. I wanted to be whole in every area. I wanted to be someone who was consumed by grace and kindness, not anger and wrath. I gave and I believed.

The changes were not noticeable at first. It actually took years and years to turn all the damaging words I believed about myself around, but I kept at it. I would drive around and pray over my city. I was at church every time it opened. I completely immersed myself in the ministry of serving with children and teens, and I continued to pour the Word in.

JOHN AVANZINI

I was teaching fifth grade in Albuquerque and had volunteered to be the advisor for the Student Counsel, comprised of third through fifth graders. One of our activities was to raise money to buy a stoplight for the lunch room. The light would show a green light when the noise level was acceptable and move to red when it got too loud. I thought it was pretty cool, so we got busy on a fundraiser. We went with a program that had trinkets and items the kids could sell. The people would order and pay for the items, then we would order them, and the kids would distribute them when they came in.

All was going well until one parent paid with a check that bounced. The order had already been placed. The amount was around $36, but it was $36 I didn't have. I immediately called the bank listed, but the woman had emptied and closed her account an hour before I called. I tried calling the phone number on the check, but it was disconnected. I talked to the student who had taken the order, but that was also a dead end. I didn't know what to do next. Certainly, my budget (the one I kept in my head because I sure didn't have any of my finances written down on paper!) would be affected that month. A few weeks went by.

One morning while I was getting ready for school, I had the Christian television station on and a man named John Avanzini was talking. He was sharing about how God is interested in helping us find lost things and things that have been stolen from us. I perked up and came closer to listen. He shared a story of how he had unknowingly lost a credit card when he was shopping at the mall in Southern California. He didn't know he was missing the card until he got the bill a month later and there were numerous charges that ended up totaling a couple thousand dollars. He immediately cancelled the card, got the charges taken care of, prayed and called the angels to work on his behalf to bring back what was stolen, then forgot about it.

A few months later he got a phone call from a young gal. She explained that she was the one who had found his card at the mall.

She and her friends had been excited to try to use it, found it was a good card and did some shopping. Then, when she was leaving the mall, she tossed it in a dumpster. Her friends asked her why she had thrown it away since it was a good card and no questions had been asked. She didn't know why, but it was no big deal to her. She also forgot about it until she turned on the TV one day and, as she was flipping through channels, saw John Avanzini's name under his picture as he was talking. She was incredulous and felt compelled to call him and let him know what had happened. She apologized and had an encounter with the God who loves her. She made things right.

I loved this story and I thought, *Why not? Why not do this with the situation with the student counsel money?* When John Avanzini led people in prayer for restoration of lost and stolen things, I joined in.

A week later, I was sitting in a teacher's meeting before school, and the secretary came in and pulled me out. She was so excited. She said, "*Just wait until you see THIS!*" She took me to the office and showed me an envelope addressed to the school that she had just opened. Inside was a cashier's check for $36 and a letter explaining that this was for the student counsel fundraiser items the woman had received but hadn't paid for. The school secretary and I were practically in tears as we knew this was God's goodness and a very real, very tangible answer to prayer.

Psalm 32:8 says, "*I will instruct you and teach you in the way which you should go; I will counsel you with My eye upon you*" (ESV). This has been my life. This is the way He has led me out of lack and darkness into His light. I love the way He leads–subtle yet so effective!

ALMOST STOLEN

I was directing and managing a children's ministry in my Foursquare Church during my teaching years. Part of my passion was to pray with my team so God's presence would saturate the ministry. We would meet once a week to pray heaven to earth. These were always powerful times; so powerful that there was great supernatural demonic resistance. One day, I arrived at school, unlocked my classroom door and saw that the room had been broken into. There was broken glass from several windows and a few games had been taken from the classroom. I knew this had to do with the prayer power that was being released as we prayed week after week for God's will to be done in our city, and for direction for the ministry. The devil didn't like it and was trying to intimidate me to stop. But I didn't.

The next attack came when my nice, new car was almost stolen. It was the day I was to go to the university for a study session for my master's degree comprehensive examination. I had planned to zip over after teaching school to join my group for an intensive study time. I walked out to my car, opened the door, got in and reached out to put the key into the ignition. But the ignition switch was gone–I couldn't start the car! I freaked out, ran to the school office, and we called the police. Sure enough, my car had been targeted to be stolen. The thieves had begun the process, but for some reason the plan had failed, and the car was still parked in the school lot. I missed my study session (I did pass my comps the next week though), but at that point I realized how serious this prayer business was, not only to the heart of God, but also to the demonic realm. I believed that the angels of

God had shown up just as the thieves were ready to jump my car and drive it away, so they were completely stopped.

My prayer team immediately began praying and calling the things in darkness to be brought to the light. (Luke 8:17) A week later, my principal called me into her office and showed me a newspaper article she had just happened to see the night before. The police had caught a car thieving ring just a couple blocks from our school. They had been stealing cars in the area and shipping them down to Mexico. Because of the covering hand of God, my car was spared, the thieving ring was caught, and justice was given for the entire community. I was so grateful and saw again the power of connection with His heart, believing His word and speaking it out over myself, my life, and any ministry He would call me to.

HOUSESITTING BLESSINGS

Another morning, while getting ready for school, John Avanzini began talking about Malachi 3:10 where God says, *"Bring the whole tithe into the storehouse, that there may be food in my house. Test me in this,"* says the LORD Almighty, *"and see if I will not throw open the floodgates of heaven and pour out so much blessing that there will not be room enough to store it"* (NIV).

As I was living month-to-month financially and it seemed that there was never enough for rent, food, gas, car payment, utilities and all, I decided to put this verse into practice. I took $50 and gave it in my church offering. I had always tithed faithfully as that is what I had been taught—the first 10% belongs to God—but I had never given above that amount as I didn't think I had it to give. But that month,

I sacrificed and gave the $50. Two weeks later, a leader at church connected me with a gal who was a pharmaceutical rep. She was single, about ten years older than me, and very well off. She needed a house sitter for a week while she was out of town on the job. I took her up on the house sitting and she paid me $200–for one week! I was shocked, and I knew this was God showing me His Word works and that this increase was directly related to the $50 I had given. I was learning about sowing and reaping.

There were several families I housesat for in this period. Since I was single and a bit older, I was trusted to take care of properties for friends when they traveled. One summer, I stayed at the house of a gal who had attended Rhema Bible Training Center in Tulsa, Oklahoma. Her bookshelves were filled with tapes, books, and recordings of all the classes she had taken. I spent all my spare time just pouring over those teachings on faith, miracles, and the power in the Word of God. It was amazing and such an opportunity that I knew God had given me.

One summer, I took care of the kids of a pastor I knew. He and his wife had also attended Rhema and had more resources including books and tapes from their classes there. I was asked to organize a closet when I was there, and that's when I found this treasure trove of teaching. I asked if I could borrow the tapes and books. They said I could.

This was another opportunity God was giving me to renew my mind and give me hope about the future. One of the most important lessons I was given during this time was about sowing and reaping, seedtime and harvest. I learned that the entire earth operates on the premise of planting seed, tending the growth, and receiving a harvest. It is set up so that when we sow, either in the natural or spiritual, good seed or bad, it will grow and there will be a harvest ... first the blade, then the ear, then the full corn in the ear. (Mark 4:28) It's a law in the earth that will never fail, like the law of gravity or the law of lift or any other physical law. It's a spiritual law and just as powerful or more powerful than natural law. And while it is working, it re-aligns and adjusts us to become more like Him, because God is the ultimate Giver and He is in every bit of giving we do. The reason we give is not to "get" but to trust and obey Him, to become more like Him and have His heart for the world. He was showing me that He is truly who He says He is. He is in the restoring and miracle-working business, and His desire was and always will be to restore me! I was seeking God in every way that I knew how.

ELLENSBURG

My first connections to Ellensburg came in the early 1980s. My sister and her husband had moved to this community in the Pacific Northwest and lived in Ellensburg for several years. My brother also came and attended Central Washington University. From time to time, I would come and visit, as would my parents. We got to know some of the locals and, during several of those times, my family became connected with the Swanstrums. My brother lived with Clint Swanstrum and his mother, Doris, while he was at the university. They all attended the same Baptist church.

The time came for my sister and her family to move back to Arizona for a season. They threw a big going away party to say goodbye to the community. I was visiting them in Ellensburg at the time of this party. For the big group of people they expected, they needed me to get tables and chairs from their church and transport them to their house. Clint was available to help, so I recruited him and we got the tables and chairs. I was charmed by his quirky humor and sense of fun. After picking up the tables, he told me that to pay him for his help, I could make him a pie.

As I flew back to Albuquerque, I told the Lord, '*Clint is the kind of guy I would like to marry.*' I loved that he played volleyball as did I, that he was fun, funny, and good looking. But I was just beginning my master's degree and teaching career, and I was enjoying living in the big city. I knew I was six years older than Clint and thought that might be a problem. I also told the Lord that I didn't want to live in "podunk" Ellensburg. I really didn't want to move back into a small community with nothing fun to do.

But I did go to multiple stores to try to find a little pie magnet for Clint's fridge that I could send him as a joke. I couldn't find one, but found a little chocolate cake magnet instead. I packaged it up with a cute note and sent it to Clint. And I never heard back from him. So that was that.

EMERSON ELEMENTARY

After teaching several years in Albuquerque schools, I ended up at Emerson Elementary School in a rough part of town known as the *War Zone*. The schools in that area had an 85% turn-over rate. I would begin my year with a class of thirty-five students and by the end of the year, 85% of the original students were gone and others had taken their place. It was a difficult school on many levels, but I was financially secure and had complete health insurance for the first time in my life.

At this school, I had a co-teacher named Paul. Paul had some savvy where finances and retirement were concerned. He had signed up for the matching funds retirement plan with the school district and shared what he had done. I couldn't understand how he could possibly live on a teacher's salary where more than the required retirement was being taken out. I wish I had followed his example, but I felt I was already living month-to-month and just didn't know how I could cut back on expenses even more. I had bought an expensive car and had car payments, but I didn't have the understanding how that could have been part of my budgeting problem. I wanted to be cool, and I really liked the car too much to think about the long-term effects of that car payment on my future.

When I left the school district, my brother-in-law encouraged me to look into taking my retirement with me by rolling it over into an IRA so there would be no fines or fees. He helped me set it all up because I had no idea what to do. I went with his suggestions and then just forgot about it. I had $11,000 in that retirement account, but I never added to it, which in retrospect would have been a smart thing to do. Thankfully God can take our 'stupid' and bring us into wisdom, which is what happened to me over the next twenty years.

Chapter 3

A FRESH START

$\mathcal{B}y$ 1990, I was teaching at a Christian school in Tucson, Arizona. I had taken a pay cut to take the job because my school in Albuquerque was going the progressive route of year-round school. This was something I didn't want to do.

The year in Tucson was a good year. I co-taught fifty-two sixth graders with an awesome, seasoned teacher, Jerry. Jerry saw the gold in me and drew it out. He continually told me how amazed he was with my creativity, passion, and ability. As a result, I thrived. Jerry really pushed me to my limits, though.

At the end of each year, the sixth graders went to a camp in the mountains. We planned for a week's stay, had activities, sports, Bible teaching, campfires, and more. I was in charge of arts and crafts; Jerry was in charge of sports and administration. He had done this camp many times.

A month or so before camp, Jerry informed me that I was going to be the Bible teacher for the week. I freaked out and told him I couldn't do it. It had been a tough year for me with the students and their families because the teacher I had replaced was well-loved and pretty much the opposite of me in personality and style. She was very loving and connecting. I'm a complete justice person. I went straight to business and expected cooperation and hard work from the students. They didn't always comply. The biggest problem was the parents. Many of them didn't want their students to fail in any way and would try to cover and protect them at any cost. This was the first time I encountered "helicopter" parents. They were constantly "hovering" to try to keep their children from any kind of failure. So there was friction between me and some of them.

I knew that if I taught the evening Bible sessions for the camp week, we could have trouble since I'm a pretty straight-shooter. But God had given me the mom of one of the students to support me. Her name was Kathy. Her husband played hockey for one of the Canadian Hockey League teams. He would play hockey in Canada, then return to Tucson once hockey season was over. Kathy was the volunteer art teacher for the third through eighth grade students. She was pretty chill, spacey, and hippie-like. Behind her back, many of the teachers made fun of her, including my co-teacher. She was just too "out there" for them.

One evening, I received a call from Kathy on my home phone. I had purposely left my home phone number out of the staff/student and parent directory because of the difficulties with the parents. I asked her how she got my number and she said she had just looked it up in the student directory. I told her it wasn't there. I looked, and it wasn't. This was the moment when I knew that this lady had a supernatural gifting about her and God wanted her in my life in a deeper way.

The next thing I knew, she came to my apartment with a bag full of groceries—I had never told her I had been struggling to make it financially. By this time, I had sold my fancy car to save money and was using my brother's old truck while he was doing mission work in South America.

Not only did Kathy show up at my door with groceries, but she had also bought socks for me and other clothing items. She didn't know, except by God, that I had need of all of it. As we visited, I shared with her that I had to teach the evening Bible services at the camp and that I didn't want to. We began praying together weekly. We declared things in prayer that we expected to happen. I was well aware of the power of the tongue and how what we speak can be a creative force. Some of my go-to verses were Job 22:28 *"You will also declare a thing, and it will be established for you; so light will shine on your ways"* (NKJV) and Romans 4:17b *"...the God, who gives life to the dead and calls those things which do not exist as though they did"* (NKJV). I knew that when I prayed and spoke in faith, the thing I spoke would happen.

Kathy and I prayed and created! One of the things we prayed was that this group of sixth graders would be so respectful (something they were not throughout the year) and so honoring that the camp director would say he had never had such an amazing group of students. God also gave me the teaching I would do for the week. He brought to my mind a song we used to sing as kids:

Jesus and others and you

What a wonderful way to spell JOY

Jesus and others and you

In the heart of each girl and each boy

J - is for Jesus, for He has first place

O - is for others we meet face-to-face

Y – is for you in whatever you do

Put yourself third and spell JOY. (Metzger 1951)

I felt Him telling me to take the first night and talk about relationship with JESUS, present the plan of salvation and call the kids to make a commitment to Him. It had been pretty evident throughout the year at this Christian school that most of the kids had never had a personal relationship with Jesus. I had night number one down.

The second night was for OTHERS. God had me pull up scripture after scripture of how God wants us to treat one another. I knew this would be convicting because so many of the problems throughout the year were a result of kids bad mouthing one another, petty jealousies, and meanness.

The third night was YOU, all about seeing yourself as God sees you, that because of the sacrifice of Jesus, we are accepted in Him and called to a higher standard. As we see ourselves through His eyes, we will act differently from the world, we will care for ourselves and others. I had had a lot of experience with this one, walking out of rejection and self-loathing to see myself as His daughter, whole and beloved. I still had a way to go, but I could speak from a place of confidence.

The final night I felt God wanted me to talk about the gifts and callings of God in Romans 12. These I referred to as the motivational gifts. What motivates us as we live our life to love and serve our family, to love and serve others and ourselves? I had a simple test for them to take as well.

Because of all the prayer from Kathy, myself and others (there were some parents who wanted to see their kids encounter Jesus), Jesus showed up and kids encountered Him. The camp director came up to Jerry and told him in all twenty plus years of running camp, he had never had a group so respectful and honoring. The kids were thanking him daily. It was amazing! Our prayers and declarations over this class were answered.

After we got back to school and the kids went back home, Jerry began getting reports of changed lives. Parents were literally crying because their kids were taking the garbage out, cleaning their rooms, and speaking respectfully to their parents. As a result, a few weeks later at the end of the year, Jerry and I each received over $350 from the parents. Traditionally, all the parents in all the grades (Kindergarten through eighth grade, two classes each level) would give towards a fund to bless the teachers. The whole fund would be divided up between all the teachers and it would typically be about $50 per teacher. But the sixth grade parents went to the principal and asked that they could specifically give their portion only to Jerry and myself. It was the miracle-working hand of God. I so saw this as His favor on me (and Jerry) for taking a stand for righteousness and justice when it wasn't the popular thing to do. I had caught another important aspect of His heart. And He had greatly blessed me financially as a result.

A SUPERNATURAL MOMENT

By this time, it had been five years since I had had the word from God that my marriage was coming and I must wait for it. I continued watching and waiting while taking the next steps in front of me. I had finished my master's degree and was teaching, but I felt a burnout coming. I had switched teaching jobs from a public school to the Christian school thinking that change would be satisfying to my soul. I was trying to hear from God and be where He wanted me to be.

One day about a month before Christmas, I was sitting at the dining room table in my apartment writing out Christmas cards. I was filling out the addresses on the envelopes when all of a sudden, I had the strangest feeling. I remember whose address I was writing—family friends, Gerry and Tianne —when this surreal sense came over me that I was writing out wedding invitations. It was such a strong feeling that I was fully expecting the man of my dreams to show up the next day! That didn't happen, so I continued teaching, doing the thing that was in front of me, but with a newly awakened expectation and excitement inside.

But my heart was waning with my teaching career. It was a scary place to be because I had spent all those years obtaining the degrees and experience in teaching, but my heart just wasn't in it anymore. I began seeking God in earnest as to what He would have me do the next year. Every spring, schools send out a form for teachers to sign about their commitment to teach for the upcoming year. I knew that was coming and a decision would have to be made. I just wasn't sure what to do.

I'M GOING TO FIND YOU A HUSBAND!

Then the unthinkable happened. In January of 1992, a family friend, Ernie, who was my parents' age, was killed in a tragic traffic accident. It was heart wrenching for me and our whole community. The sadness was a continuation of the previous spring when his son, who was my age, passed away suddenly and unexpectedly with a brain aneurism. These folks were a founding family of the area where my parents lived and where I spent my teen years. Their name was known throughout the region. In fact, the Trading Post, Vanderwagen, New Mexico was named after their family of homesteaders years before. They were connected and well-loved traders of Indian jewelry. Ernie could speak the languages of two tribes, Navajo and Zuni, and was well-loved by so many. The funeral took place at the end of January in Gallup, New Mexico. I was devastated and barely made it through the service. I just leaned on my dad and cried and cried. Ernie had been a loving father figure for me. He had loved me.

After the service, we went to the Vanderwagen homestead for the post-funeral reception. I visited with Ernie's wife, Esther, and she told me she was going to leave the Southwest for a time. It was just too difficult having been married to Ernie for forty years and to remain living in the area where everyone knew them. She needed some time away. She and Ernie had planned to go on the road that summer to sell Indian jewelry at several big jewelry trade shows. She was planning on keeping to the schedule. She asked me if I would like to come along with her. Immediately my heart said a resounding, *Yes*! So it was settled. I would go on the road selling jewelry with Esther. She joked with me saying, "*I'm going to find you a husband and get you married!*" That was just fine by me.

The end of the school year came, and because I was scared to launch into the unknown, I went ahead and signed the intent to teach form for the next school year. Then I hit the road with Esther and her little dog, Hillary.

HOUSTON, SALT LAKE CITY, SEATTLE

The first stop was Houston, Texas, and I hated it. We stayed at the flea-infested house of a friend of Esther's. It was horrible. Esther's dog was infested with fleas, and we both had flea bites all over our ankles. It was really not a great start.

I was taking the travel opportunity to ask God where He wanted me to be. I was using my "spiritual radar" to test my spiritual connection with each place we travelled. In my mind and heart, it was kind of like playing the Hot/Cold game where one player selects a household item for hiding and a second player searches for it slowly and deliberately while the first player assists with verbal clues. If the searching player is not at all close to the item in the search, the first player says, "*You're cold,*" but as he gets closer to the hidden item, the response is, "*Getting warmer...*" When the player is very close to the item, the first player will say, "*You're hot!*" The verbal temperature indicators aid in finding the item. This is what I would do, but inside my head. I just had a gut feeling and I could sense if I was hot, warm or cold. Even though temperature-wise it was hot in Houston, it was icy cold for me spiritually, and I knew it was not where I needed to land.

The next show we did was in Salt Lake City, Utah. It was a fun show. I met lots of people. Esther was very friendly with all the other exhibitors and was a mom figure to me. She took care of me very well. I did the grunt work of setting up and tearing down the booth along with some selling of the jewelry we had brought. Salt Lake City felt a little "warmer" to me, but I knew it also wasn't the place God wanted me to be.

We continued our northward trek to Seattle. But first, I asked Esther if we could stop in Roslyn, Washington, which was the set for the popular TV show, "Northern Exposure." I had a friend in New Mexico who loved the show and I wanted to take some pictures to send to him. It was a small town. We were through it quickly and traveling on to Seattle. There I continued my quest with God and felt that I was closer to the place God had next for me.

After our show, Esther's plan was to return to New Mexico, but since the stop in Roslyn, she had been thinking and had a change of heart. She decided to go back to Roslyn and see if she could open a Southwest Indian jewelry shop there. Her hope was to have a break from the tight-knit community in her Southwest world so she could grieve her husband's death at her own pace. She told me to take two weeks and figure out something to do during that time so she could take stock and see about opening a shop in Roslyn.

FINALLY!

My future sister-in-law lived near Seattle an hour or so away from Roslyn. I gave her a call, she picked me up, and we hung out for two weeks. She had attended Central Washington University in Ellensburg where she met my brother when they both were in college there. As we had a weekend between my two weeks of travel respite, we decided to take a trip to Ellensburg where the college is located. My sister-in-law wanted to visit her church, the local Ellensburg Christian Missionary Alliance church (CMA), and my brother's church, one of the Baptist churches in town. We arrived at the first service of the CMA church and I knew right away that this was not the place God was calling me for the next season. But Ellensburg and the surrounding area felt at home to me. It just felt right. Then we went to the service at the Baptist church.

We walked in the door of the church. Immediately, I knew this is where God wanted me to be and that I would be moving to Ellensburg soon. It had been six years since I had been there and had seen Clint Swanstrum. He was standing up at the front of the sanctuary near the piano. When he saw us, he immediately got a huge grin on his face, came right over and said, "*You still owe me a pie!*" I laughed and laughed. He was so funny! Neither of us knew if the other one was in a relationship or even married. But there was still a lot of fun there.

My sister-in-law later asked me what I thought of Clint and me in a potential relationship. I wondered if anyone really knew him at all. She said even though they were all in the Christian college group together while at CWU, Clint was just the funny one and no one really knew him. She issued a challenge to see if I could get Clint aside sometime and have him talk about himself for one-half hour. I love a good challenge, so I took it! But it would be several months before I could engage in the challenge.

THE CHALLENGE

Esther and I finished our trip with Esther deciding to pack up in New Mexico and move to Roslyn, Washington for a season. I made the decision to end my teaching contract the Christian school in Tucson. I went back to my parents' place with the intention of moving to Ellensburg since that is where I felt God wanted me to be.

Meanwhile, my brother had returned to New Mexico from his missions work in Bolivia and was headed north to Washington. My future sister-in-law was with him. They invited me to join them on the trip. I had sold my car when I was teaching in Tucson to save money and had been using my brother's old truck. Now I had no vehicle, no job, and pretty much no money to my name. I joined them in going north.

When we got to Ellensburg, my sister-in-law suggested I call Clint's mother and ask her if I could stay with them a few nights. I called. Clint answered the phone and I asked if I could stay with them while I waited for my brother and sister-in-law to finish their business in Ellensburg. Later, I learned that the day I called, August 21, was Clint's birthday, and when I asked him if I could stay, he told himself, "*Happy Birthday to Me!*" and of course he said yes.

It was a Sunday evening when I arrived at the farm, so Clint's mom was in town at church. It was just Clint and me. I figured this was the perfect time to get Clint to talk for thirty minutes and win the challenge my sister-in-law had given me. I launched into my questions. Clint was so easy to talk to! He was comfortable, answered all my questions, and talked for two hours. At one point about an hour in, I saw a picture of two large barn doors opening up until they were completely open, and I heard the Holy Spirit say, "*The doors are open if you want to go through.*" I instantly knew that this was about moving forward in relationship with this man.

In my thirty-seven years, I had never had God release me to any relationship. I had plenty of experience going forward on my own, which had never ended well. This time, the difference was stunning. I didn't tell Clint what I saw, but he was open to moving forward in relationship. At that point, it was clear to me that I would move to Washington to see what God had in store.

YEAR OF CHANGES

Clint's mom, Doris, owned the farm where Clint had grown up. He had been living with her on the farm until five years before when she moved to a family house in town seven miles away. The house in town had belonged to Clint's aunt and uncle. After they both had passed away, in order for Doris to take ownership of the house, she had to live in it for three out of the next five years.

When I arrived in September 1992, Doris was coming to the end of her three required years and was planning on moving back to the farm in December. Clint's Aunt Iona really wanted him to get married, so she had given him her green Ford LTD (Clint called it a *courtin' car*) and her wedding ring. She didn't want thirty-year-old

Clint living with his mother any longer. The whole family wanted him to find the "one" and get married to carry on the Swanstrum name.

Upon moving to Ellensburg, I moved into the house in town with Clint's mom. I started a job doing transcription work for Central Washington Comprehensive Mental Health (CWCMH). I was greatly relieved to have a break from teaching. Ellensburg was a small town, so I could walk to work and just slow my life down. I was finally ready to live in this small town.

Clint and I began dating and enjoyed getting to know each other. My mom and Clint's mom were both very eager for us to get engaged and married. There was a lot of pressure as I was already thirty-seven and he was thirty-one. But Clint wasn't ready to take that next step, so we entered into pre-engagement counseling with our church pastor. I had never heard of pre-engagement counseling but was willing to give it a try since it promised to move our relationship forward.

By June, the proposal came. I said yes, and we began all over again, this time with engagement counseling. We covered all the bases, for sure. I was continuing to work for CWCMH, making enough to live on but not thinking of the future. I was not saving anything, and I had no insurance or retirement savings. But I was a giver. There were times I would give half my paycheck to someone in need. I was always looking for places I could give. I was practicing hearing Jesus' voice and giving when I felt He said to give. I figured giving was great training ground for me to learn to hear Him better and that if I missed it, there wouldn't be much damage done as giving is always from the heart of God!

VBS

I began attending the little Baptist church Clint and his mom attended. It was perplexing to me that after all the years God had been teaching me about the spiritual realm and how my gifts and callings fit in, I would now be back in a church that taught none of those things. But I knew this was where God wanted me to be and, by now, I was coming to understand that God has seasons of life. This was just a new season for me.

I had tons of experience working in children's ministries, had put on Vacation Bible Schools with carnival events, taught weekly kids' church services, and worked with children's ministry teams in various churches and ministries. I felt the hand of God leading me to engage with the kids in this little Baptist church. There were about twenty-five regular kids in the children's ministry. I jumped right in. My hope was to put on an awesome VBS that first summer, bringing many un-churched kids to Jesus. I cleared it with the pastor and began planning.

As I had a full-time job and there was only a very small budget for any kids' ministry through the church, I began using my own money to buy supplies, curriculum, prizes, decorations, and everything that would be needed for an awesome VBS. I had a big vision, and I knew it would be more expensive than what this church would be able to understand and fund. I poured well over $1,000 into that first VBS, but doing so made my heart sing!

Before I put any plan into motion, I started a weekly prayer gathering to pray over this VBS. I knew the power of prayer. I had seen so many times in my life that when I prayed, things happened. I especially knew this to be true when it came to bringing children to Jesus and pouring His love and fun on them. Jesus loves kids! I took James 5:16 literally, "*The effectual fervent prayer of a righteous man avails much, makes tremendous power available, dynamic in its working*" (KJV & AMPC).

Somehow, I had an understanding of the love of God toward children, and as I tapped into His heart, He would move and meet every need. Three months ahead of the scheduled summer VBS, I announced that we would begin having a weekly prayer time. This would be open to anyone in the church and especially the volunteers who wanted to be part of the summer program. The first week there were three people, me, Clint's mom, Doris, and one other lady. The next week our group became just Doris and me. I was so grateful that Doris was faithful. She was there to pray with me every week and it made a huge difference.

I had told the church I was believing for seventy-five kids to come to our VBS. There were those who scoffed at that "high" number. The week came for the kick-off and we decorated and prepared. There were plenty of volunteers for all the classes and age groups. As the decorations went up, excitement grew. The week was going to end with a big carnival on Friday evening where the kids could spend the VBS Bucks they had earned during the week and have their whole family join in the fun.

The first day we had 75 kids show up. Every day, more and more would come as the word got out. Even the long-time church people who had not seen a VBS in their church for years began to get excited. Their hope, joy and expectation rose significantly. There was a buzz around the whole church as to what was happening. By Friday, we had 109 kids registered and attending. Kids were receiving Jesus, worshiping, and having the time of their lives. It was well worth the cost—physically and financially.

But once again, there was that discouraging kick-back. One of the women who volunteered with the Vacation Bible School came up to me at the close of the week. Although she enjoyed ministering to the kids and seeing families touched and blessed, she told me I was too much. She told me that I did things too big, my vision was too large for this valley and for others in the church. She didn't like it at all that I had such an expansive vision and life. I had to fight in my heart against the wave of discouragement those words brought.

On the Sunday following VBS, Pastor Fred spoke to the congregation about the woman who brought the costly perfume and poured it on Jesus' feet. Pastor Fred had bought an $80 bottle of perfume and poured it out into a pan in front of a fan as he spoke so the fragrance filled the room. He told the people that what had happened this week of VBS was a joy and pleasure to God as we gave it all to see kids brought to Jesus. He had had some folks grumble to him throughout the VBS planning and implementing process that it was too extravagant, too much work, and too big. Pastor Fred did not agree. He was thrilled with the results. He saw the kiss of God on everything we did and received it all with open arms.

Needless to say, we continued having VBS for several summers after that, and we welcomed the kids from far and wide. People's hearts were slowly changed from the "Us Four and No More" poverty mentality of never having enough to living with an open hand and reaching out to a community hungry for Jesus.

CWCMH

I was thoroughly enjoying my transcription job at Central Washington Comprehensive Mental Health. It was wonderful to be away from the pressure and stress of teaching, to just have a job I could go to and leave it there when I went home. When I began the job, I worked out of the main office on 4th Street, but soon was moved to a small house in town that the organization had purchased for office space. I typed all the intakes of those coming in for counseling as well as the case notes for the case managers. Many of the case managers worked with foster kids and the foster care families in the community.

I was told that our county had the highest number of abused and neglected foster kids in the state. I saw that firsthand when typing the case notes. Many days I would be in tears as I typed what the case managers had seen and what these kids had experienced. I soon saw that this was another "ministry" God was handing to me. I could pray over each one as I typed. I was the "fly on the wall," seeing from a distance what was happening in their homes and in their hearts. It was such a privilege to be able to pray over them. At times I thought that perhaps I might be the only one praying for each individual. I was needed and asked to do a job by my Father. It was my honor to obey.

Chapter 4

A YEAR OF FIRSTS

I_n the fall, October 16, 1993, Clint and I were married. I was so happy to finally be married to a wonderful guy, and I just wanted to enjoy several years together before any children came along. However, I was thirty-eight, and the family pressure was on for getting those grandbabies coming. Both my mom and Doris, Clint's mom, pointed out a number of times that the biological clock was ticking. Doris really wanted a boy to carry on the Swanstrum name, as did the rest of Clint's family. Their plan was not necessarily our plan!

BUYING THE FARM

Clint's mom had expected Clint to take over the farm, and when we got married, she decided it was time to sell it to us. Clint had worked for her the previous thirteen years, keeping the farm in good order after his dad died. His mom figured that value into the sale price as she wrote up the contract. Several years earlier, she had also had Clint take out an insurance policy for her. She wanted him to easily be able to buy his three sisters out of the family property when she passed away.

Clint purchased a whole life insurance policy for $100,000. He paid the monthly premiums, and by the time I came into his life, he had paid $30,000 on the policy. We had no understanding of how whole life insurance versus term life worked, but fortunately in Clint and Doris' case, it turned out well. We came into an awareness of the benefits of term life and the pitfalls of whole life some years later. God was watching out for all of us.

Clint had a desire and a *knowing* that we would pay the farm off in seven years. I had no problem with that, although I was extremely frustrated that we never seemed to have money to do anything extra such as go out to eat, vacation, or buy new clothes and household furnishings. We had enough and weren't in a financial crisis, but it always seemed that we only had *just* enough.

Clint was working for a guy who built houses, and as he worked side by side with Eric, he was learning the building trade, although not making much money. I was working a forty-hour week as well at minimum wage. We were chunking all our money at the farm debt, with Clint being more determined than I was to pay it off in that seven-year period. Financially we were inching along.

ANOTHER PROMISE

In January of 1995, I found I was pregnant with our daughter, Kelcy, due in October. It was a little too soon for my plan, but the grandmas were ecstatic. That spring, Clint and I went to a Hosanna! Music worship conference in Portland, Oregon. While there, we attended a workshop called, "*Leading Worship in the Small Church.*" The room was packed with over fifty people. It was led by Marty Nystrom, a worship leader and song writer well-known for the worship chorus he had written, *As the Deer.*

In the class, he demonstrated how to lead worship very simply from a keyboard, integrating scripture reading and prayer, and giving people a chance to be part of the service. Then he began to prophesy over people in the room. He called to Clint and me and he said, "*God is using you as a TEAM. Your ministry is as a couple. People are watching you closely and even though there may be some situations where there is jealousy, the Lord is allowing you to cut through the jealousy. It is coming off of you like water off a duck's back. These are attacks from the evil one, but you won't let them phase you. People say, 'Everything goes right for them!' You will be ministering to couples and families, and the ministry you are entering into is greater than anything so far.*"

When he finished, I was in tears, again. This was exactly what my heart wanted, and again God was showing me He heard my heart's cry. He was faithful to bring it to pass. But there was one thing that was confusing to me. We were deeply involved in children's ministry and that was all I had ever done. I had taught elementary school and junior high. I had also worked in youth ministry with high schoolers, but never adults, couples, and families. I wasn't sure how that could possibly play out, so I just hid that word in my heart, wrote it out for my declarations list, and moved on.

YOUNG FAMILY

On October 8, 1995, after two years of marriage, our daughter was born. I was forty years old having my first child. It truly was a miraculous birth. God's hand was on every moment, and the sense of His presence was at times overwhelming. In fact, at one point in the labor process, our friend, Marilyn, was warming up some soup on the stove for me. As the labor intensified, so did the electric burner. It kept burning hotter and hotter until it completely burned out and the stove was ruined. Shortly after that, Kelcy made her entrance. And I got a new stove!

It took me a bit to adjust to being a new mom this late in the game, but I found I enjoyed it immensely. I had pulled out of all children's ministry and kept working at my job, but was able to take my baby with me, and I enjoyed all the new things I was experiencing and learning. The most amazing thing to me was how much I loved my daughter, and I kept thinking over and over about my mom and how she had communicated that she didn't like me. I couldn't understand that any mom could decide to not love their child. I was smitten with my little girl and loved being a little family together.

When Kelcy was four years old, we stretched ourselves and began hosting students from the Asia University America Program (AUAP) through Central Washington University in our town. I had been raised in a multicultural environment as a missionary's kid in New

Mexico and felt living with cultures different than my own had greatly enhanced my understanding and ability to honor other ways of thinking and doing life. I wanted the same for my daughter.

Through the AUAP, we were able to become Community Friends two times a year, each for a five-month period, with two Japanese students each time. The students would come from Asia University in Japan to live and study in the U.S. for five months. They were eager to experience the dynamics of American families and as much as they could of American life. We were counseled to take girl students because they were more relational and were told that they loved to be Community Friends with families who had small children. We found this to be true, and we enjoyed many cycles of beautiful friendships with Japanese students who became part of our family.

DON'T YOU KNOW YOU CAN HAVE WHAT YOU SAY!

This was a period of time where our giving extended outside our own families, outside of our church giving, and we began to have a heart for the nations. We loved hanging out with these girls, cooking Japanese food, learning to make sushi, going shopping, playing games, riding horses, and making apple cider. We opened up our home and hearts completely to them. It was another way for us to freely give the love of Jesus to the world. We could do it without having to travel anywhere!

Along with our giving, my declaring God's promises over our family increased. Daily for at least forty minutes, I would walk around our house speaking His Word. I wasn't sure if it had any effect, but I knew I should keep doing it because I knew I had what I said. I was retraining my mind to think like God thought. I understood sowing and reaping very well and knew that it takes time for a crop to grow.

But I do remember how disheartening it was when I had spoken blessing and life over our farm, cattle, fields, and household from Deuteronomy 28 and then a cow or horse would randomly die. I would feel like I had failed in my task. I hadn't believed enough. I hadn't spoken enough. But even with the disappointment of losing cattle or horses, which happened probably six times over our twenty-seven years together, I still knew that God's promises were truer than my circumstances and I kept going, kept speaking, kept declaring, kept slowly renewing my mind and increasing my faith. I knew and believed God's Word that *"So then faith comes by hearing and hearing by the Word of God"* (Romans 10:17 KJV). I was determined to have as much of the Word in my heart as I possibly could. I couldn't really track the changes, but in looking back after years and years of faithfully speaking His Word, we are now living in the abundance of all His promises. It is truly amazing to me.

Here are some of my favorite promises from Deuteronomy 28 and other sections of scripture that I spoke daily:

1. The blessing of the Lord makes us rich and He adds no sorrow to it.

2. Our lands drink water from the rain of Heaven.

3. They are lands for which the Lord our God cares.

4. The eyes of the Lord our God are always on them from the beginning even to the end of the year.

5. As we listen obediently to Him and speak His Word, as we love and serve Him with all our heart and soul, He gives rain for our lands in its season, the early and the late rain, that we may gather in our grain and our new wine and our oil.

6. He gives grass in our fields for our cattle, and we shall eat and be satisfied.

7. We honor the Lord with our possessions, and with the first fruits of all our increase;

8. Then our barns are filled with plenty and our vats overflow with new wine.

9. We obey and serve Him.

10. We spend our days in prosperity and our years in pleasures.

11. The Lord has brought us out into a place of rich fulfillment.

12. We are His servants and the Lord takes pleasure in our prosperity.

13. All these blessings come on us and overtake us.

14. We are blessed in the city and blessed in the country.

15. Blessed are our offspring - Kelcy and Casey.

16. Blessed is the produce of our ground.

17. Blessed is the offspring of our beasts, the increase of our herd, and the young of our flock.

18. Blessed is our basket and kneading bowl.

19. We are blessed coming in and blessed going out.

20. We are the head and not the tail.

21. We are above and not beneath.

Recently I was told of a dream that a minister named Abner Suarez shared awhile back. He said he had a dream one night where he was seated around a table of people who were leaders in the U.S. church. Jesus was there. He walked up to Abner and stood right in front of him. Jesus then said to him, "*Don't you know you can have what you say?*" Abner said, "*Well, yes, of course Lord, that's how we started the ministry.*"

Jesus leaned in closer and put his hands on Abner's shoulders and said louder, "*Don't you know you can have what you say?*" Again, Abner said, "*Yes, yes of course, Lord, I know.*" Then Jesus leaned in until He was only a few inches from Abner's face, held his shoulders, and shouted, "*Don't you know you can have what you say?*" and the dream ended.

I KNOW I can have what I say. I know that I DO have what I say. I have seen it in action in my life for many years and I try to keep tabs on my words when I'm not consciously declaring His Word. It is not always easy, but it is always worth it. The book of James in the New Testament talks about how powerful the tongue is. I want my tongue to be used for good and not for evil, to bring increase and blessing to my family and those around me. I will declare His Word. It is the most powerful force in the universe, and I believe it!

PAID OFF

Sadly, Clint's mom passed away in October, 1999. Kelcy was four years old, and I was pregnant with our second child. December, 1999 was the end of the seven years that Clint had believed we would have the farm completely paid off. We received the payout from the insurance policy he had been paying into for his mom. It was $100,000. We were able to completely pay off the farm. The farm payment went into Clint's mom's estate, paid off the farm completely, and the rest was split between the four siblings. Doris had also set aside $2,000 for each grandchild. I was pregnant with our second at the time, and she had even thoughtfully arranged for our coming baby to receive $2,000 from her estate.

As the siblings cleaned out Doris' house, we kept finding small caches of money in purses, jacket pockets, bathroom drawers, in small boxes stashed away, above the car visors, in the glove compartment, and stuck in kitchen drawers. It was actually quite fun and gave us a chance to process her passing, enjoy the time treasure-hunting together as family, being grateful for her generosity. All told, we dug up $4,000, so each family got an extra $1,000 cash. I don't think I had ever seen that much cash in one place in my life, and I was amazed with this family and their ability to save money as well as be completely fair and honest with one another. Everything was split evenly with no arguments, no strife or complaint. It was a totally different scenario from my mom and her family, and it required me to shift my thinking again. This time the shift was away from an entitled mentality of '*that should be mine*' to seeing equal value in each person and the importance of valuing another over self.

DWIGHT

A month or so after the insurance payout, Clint was walking out in the fields, and he felt strongly that God wanted us to give $25,000 to a friend who was fighting cancer. Dwight attended our church and was a wonderful man who had been diagnosed with an aggressive cancer. His hope was to go to Mexico to receive an alternative treatment to the normal radiation/chemotherapies. He didn't have the money to be able to go. When Clint told me he felt he had heard from God, it immediately resonated in my heart and I said, *Yes!* We quickly gave the money to Dwight and his wife, which helped with the need but also delivered a huge dose of hope.

Dwight was able to get the treatment he had hoped for, although it didn't have the desired effect, and he died shortly after. But for Clint and I to come together in agreement so early in our marriage and give such a large gift was a wonderful thing for me. I dreamed of the possibilities, of all the future giving we would do.

When I gave birth to Kelcy, I was pretty sure I never wanted to do THAT again. It was challenging becoming a first-time mom at forty. But it was wonderful, as well. I continued working at my paid job but was able to work from home part-time while Kelcy was a baby. That worked well for a couple years. Eventually I was able to quit and become a full-time stay-at-home mom. I loved it. My days were filled with loving on my little girl, declaring God's Word over every area of our lives, and being a wife and mom. I was living in the promises I had been believing for years. It was wonderful.

During this time, I was a regular partner with Kenneth Copeland Ministries–a Word of Faith ministry out of Texas. This is where I had learned about faith and how to activate it in my life. It was the most amazing thing to me to read the testimonies of real people with real needs who trusted a real God and used their faith to accomplish what looked like the impossible. I began using the same principles I was learning through this ministry and began to see changes in my own circumstances. I also learned some keys for my life from another minister who worked with Kenneth Copeland. His name was Jerry Savelle and he wrote a personal memoir called *In the Footsteps of a Prophet*, published in 1999.

The book revolutionized my life in terms of giving, believing God for increase, and the desires of my heart. In the book, Jerry talked about how the Kingdom of God has a legal aspect to it. When God makes a promise, it is based on a legal system that He will uphold. There are things I must do and there are things He will do based on the covenant I have with Him as a believer in Jesus and His shed blood on the cross. Jerry introduced me to something he called a "Petition for a Heavenly Grant." This was life changing for me and Clint. Jerry had learned this through Kenneth Copeland as he had been studying John 16:23 which says, *"And when that time comes, you will ask nothing of Me [you will need to ask Me no questions]. I assure you, most solemnly I tell you, that My Father will grant you whatever you ask in My name"* (AMP).

The purpose of writing out a grant would be similar to applying for a grant for college tuition. It would represent a legal document along with being a tangible paper which would be a point of contact for faith as well as serving the purpose of helping me to stay single-minded and focused on the thing I was believing God for.

I saw the wisdom of God on this and began writing out Heavenly Grants. I was believing God for all sorts of things, from having someone to come prune our fruit trees (I tried and failed miserably, and Clint didn't have any time to do it), to having our fence along the road fixed (it was a mess from years of livestock crashing through it), to having finances to pay taxes, being able to attend God-conferences, and many more. I copied the example Jerry had put in his book and changed out his and his wife's signature lines for Clint and me. Then Clint and I went through each contract, read the scriptures we were standing on to believe God's increase over our lives, prayed, and verbally remembered together the giving we had done and that, because we had sowed, we would also reap. We dated and signed the covenant contracts and put them up where we could see them often.

As I look back twenty-one years, I am amazed how ALL our covenant contract Heavenly Grants have been fulfilled. Every. Single. One. Some took many years to see them come to pass, some less years, and some only months, but all were fulfilled. We marked each one PAID as they came to pass, and we celebrated what God had done in our lives and in our faith. We had grown so much in faith.

Below is one of our first Heavenly Grants. When I was writing it, I remember feeling very strange. I had never heard of anyone doing this kind of thing except Jerry Savelle, but it made sense to me. It felt a little bit like the 'Name it, claim it' stuff that I had heard about, but our hearts were sincere and I was doing what I knew to do to keep God's promises before my heart and in front of my eyes so my faith would be strong.

The first contract for a piano took eleven years to completely fulfill, but it was so worth it. We wanted a 'real' piano for Kelcy. When she was very young, a family needed us to keep their piano for a year, and it was so nice having a real piano in the house. Kelcy began learning to play on that piano. But when the family took their piano back, we went for an electric keyboard as we didn't have enough money to buy a real piano. When Kelcy started taking piano lessons, her teacher really wanted us to buy an authentic piano for her. But the cost for the type of piano she wanted us to get was $10,000 or higher. This was something we simply could not afford. It was actually laughable! Then one day, the teacher contacted us to let us know that she had found a piano for $800–a baby grand the former high school choir teacher had purchased for his wife thirty years before. It was a great piano, well taken care of, and in our price range. We certainly saw this as the blessing of the Lord and went for it. We still have and love this piano. What a great first contract to be fulfilled!

COVENANT CONTRACT FOR A PIANO

We, *Clint Swanstrum & Becky Swanstrum,* come to You, Father, in the Name of Jesus. We come boldly to the throne of grace according to Hebrews 4:16 as Your very own children, as the righteousness of God, with a sense of reverence but also a sense of belonging.

John 16:23 states, "And in that day ye shall ask Me nothing. Verily, verily, I say unto you, whatsoever ye shall ask the Father in My Name, He will give it to you."

Matthew 21:22 states, "If you believe, you will receive whatever you ask for in prayer."

Mark 11:24 states, "Therefore I say unto you, What things so ever ye desire, when ye pray, believe that ye receive them, and ye shall have them."

Psalm 37:4 states, "Delight yourself also in the Lord and He shall give you the desires of your heart."

And Proverbs 13:21 states, "Adversity pursues sinners, but the righteous will be rewarded with prosperity."

Your Word states in Luke 6:38, "Give and it shall be given unto you; good measure, pressed down, and shaken together, and running over, shall men give unto your bosom." In accordance with Your Word, we have given in order to set this Spiritual Law to work on our behalf. We draw on our heavenly account which is full, in Jesus' Name. According to Matthew 18:18, we bind Satan and all his forces, and we render them helpless and unable to operate. They will not hinder our Covenant Contract, and we will receive our petition answered in full.

According to Hebrews 1:13 and 14, we loose the ministering spirits, and we charge them to go forth and cause this grant to come into our hands.

We petition for a heavenly grant of $5,000 for a piano, realizing You are not broke and want to bless us. We join with the Lord God Almighty, fully expecting 100% completion of this contract, based on the Word of God, and we set ourselves in agreement according to Matthew 18:19, "Again I say unto you, that if two of you shall agree on earth as touching anything that they shall ask, it shall be done for them of My Father which is in heaven."

Signed this 2nd day of October 1999:   Contract Completed on:

Rebecca L Swanstrum   *May 25. 2010*

Clint Swanstrum $150 keyboard from Costco

$650 keyboard from Costco (9/2004)

$800 baby grand piano (5/25/2010)

PAID IN FULL!

CASEY

After a couple years, I was ready to add another child to our family, and so was Clint. But there seemed to be a fertility issue. By now I was forty-three and trying to have another baby, but it just wasn't working. We tried for a year, and just when all seemed hopeless, God spoke.

We were friends with a family who had two older elementary children and were sensing that their family wasn't complete. They wanted another child. However, they had taken steps to not become pregnant, so they were looking at adoption. God put it on our hearts to support them financially and give $1,000 toward the adoption. At this time, that amount was HUGE for us. It was greatly extravagant, but we sacrificed and saved to be able to do it.

Within two weeks of giving that gift, I was pregnant with Casey. It was so obvious that God was honoring our giving and our faith. The verse He kept before my eyes and heart at this time was Acts 10:31(ESV) where Peter was sent to Cornelius with the message "... *Cornelius, your prayer has been heard and your alms have been remembered before God.*"

I had heard a sermon where the words "remembered before God" were literally "have risen as a memorial," and the speaker said to picture the alms giving as a solid brick wall that was being built in front of God to be seen day and night. I pictured that wall in my mind of our giving over the years, and specifically of the money we gave toward our friends' adoption expenses with the faith that we would have another child of our own.

TRAIN UP

As I've said before, I loved the Old Testament characters and could relate to many of them so often. They are the great cloud of witnesses that Hebrews 12:1 speaks of. They are the ones spoken of in Hebrews chapter 11, Abraham, Enoch, Sarah, Moses, Isaac, Jacob, Gideon, Barak, Samson, Jephthah, David, and the rest. I knew as I reached out in faith, there were others, including this great cloud, pulling with and for us. During this believing in faith for our little boy, I saw myself as Hannah crying out for a son, for her Samuel, and then dedicating him to the Lord.

God had given me a strong desire that our children were to be set apart to Him. I loved that idea as I felt He had specifically set me apart even while I was in the womb in His naming of me and then in my actual birth in the car on the way to the hospital. I had no problem listening to and obeying the instruction of the Lord to set these two apart for His heart and service.

There were three areas I specifically knew we were not to take the normal path. First: We were not to involve them in the medical system—they would be born at home and would not be subject to the vaccines that hospital-born babies were. I was to stand in faith for them and us as a family to live in divine healing.

The second area was education: I was to school them at home and not send them to either public or private schools. God wanted us to shepherd their hearts during the sweet, fragile time of their childhood. I had no problem with home schooling as I had experience as a teacher in both the public and private sectors and wanted no part of the negatives I had experienced for my own children.

It was remarkable to me to see Kelcy's and Casey's gifts and interests grow and flourish as Clint and I made room for each child's interests. Kelcy loved the stage and the stage loved her. She shone when dancing, singing, and performing. Casey was highly intuitive, extremely creative, and more inward-focused. He loved experimenting and creating small things. I would constantly find creations of paper, wood, and wire hidden throughout the house. If I ever wondered where the scissors or glue were, I would go to Casey.

Even though we didn't have much residual income to put into their extracurricular activities, we always made sure they had at least one outlet where they could express themselves and grow creatively. We worked our way through horse and dog 4H, dance and piano for Kelcy. Casey dabbled in Lego 4H, creating and filming stop-motion short movies for his YouTube channel, and a bit of snowboarding. Homeschool was a great blessing and the way to go for us as we launched our children into the destinies God had for them.

The third area: We and our children were to spend our lives serving people, giving of ourselves and resources to others—whether in church, with international students, or whoever God brought into our world.

It very much felt like how God had set Sampson, the last of Israel's judges, apart as a Nazarite. God had let Sampson's parents know that he was to be to be separated and consecrated to God from birth. I felt that God wanted this for our children, but with a different twist as we are no longer living under Old Testament law, but under grace in Jesus. I determined to try my best to pour a love for Jesus into the hearts of my kids. He was first and foremost in our days, in our nights, and in every part of our lives.

My key verses during these years were:

Proverbs 22:6 (AMPC) *"Train up a child in the way he should go, and in keeping with his individual gift or bent, and when he is old, he will not depart from it."*
And Isaiah 54:13 (AMPC) *"All of your ... children shall be disciples [taught by the Lord and obedient to His will], and great shall be the peace and undisturbed composure of your children."*

I said these two verses many times over the course of my kids' growing up years, sometimes to them, sometimes to me, and sometimes to put God in remembrance of His Word, just to help get me through a particularly trying day.

KIDS CO.

Our next ministry step after the children's ministry at the Baptist church in Ellensburg was to step into children's ministry leadership at Ellensburg Foursquare Church. We did this for five years. We actually began attending the church when I was pregnant with Kelcy. I was pretty burned out from years of children's ministry in New Mexico, in Arizona, and the few years at the Baptist church. My first pregnancy as a forty-year-old had worn me out and I really wanted to remain anonymous when we began attending Foursquare.

I have heard enough God-stories of peoples' lives to realize that God moves consistently in similar ways in leading specific people, families, and individuals. With us, God picks the churches He wants us to be a part of–some are for shorter seasons, some for longer, but we are always supernaturally led by Him when it comes to our "assignment" church at any certain time. One day as I was driving by the Foursquare church, I clearly heard God say that this was the church He wanted us to attend. So we did. We would slip in the back, enjoy the service, and slip out. It was nice being able to just relax and attend church instead of being heavily involved as I had been my whole life. Kelcy was born in October 1995, and in January 1996, the church scheduled a meeting for those considering membership. As we had been attending now for four months, we thought it might be a good idea to go "just to see." While at the meeting, we filled out the forms asking what our strength serving areas were and I put down my years of experience as a children's ministry leader. Maybe something inside me wanted to get back into ministry, maybe there was some sense of guilt that I needed to be involved more, but when the call came shortly after that meeting that there was a need to run the kids' mid-week service club (Pioneer Club) for the church, I was heavily resistant.

Eventually, after talking with the pastors and giving all my excuses, I said I would at least cover for the regular gal for several months while she was out of town. I also told the leadership that I didn't want to continue the current club format. I wanted to use the children's ministry materials from Willie George's church, Church on the Move, in Tulsa, Oklahoma. This is the ministry where I received the prophecy about my marriage and ministry. I loved the life of God on that ministry, and how everything they did and all their materials were steeped in the supernatural wonder and power of God. The leadership of Foursquare agreed, and Clint was in agreement, so we started the journey.

Within a couple months, the group of thirteen kids grew to forty, and we needed a new space. We were moved from a classroom to several classrooms to house the younger age groups, and to the sanctuary for the large group. Soon we were averaging one hundred ten kids every Wednesday night. We had a volunteer base of forty adults and a fifteen-member kids' leadership team. These kids led worship, played in the band, and served the weekly attenders. We named the ministry 'The Kids Company' and called it Kids Co. This was another avenue of giving and bringing blessing to others. We personally invested heavily into the Kids Co. ministry, even buying a large bounce house for special Kids Co. Big Nights.

I was continuing to work at Comprehensive Mental Health, typing case notes for foster kids and broken families. I would just cry and pray as I typed those notes, believing God for restoration of families, and for hearts to come to Jesus. As Ellensburg is a small town, sometimes I would see the people whose notes I typed in and around town. Then, as the Foursquare children's ministry grew, some of these families began coming on Wednesday nights. I remember the feelings I had when I saw the first kids I had typed many notes about coming through the doors. It was almost overwhelming to see how God was orchestrating their freedom and connection to His heart through this tangible ministry where they and their families would be seen, where they would come to know His deep love for them, where we could take care of them in practical as well as spiritual ways.

WE LIVE TO GIVE AND WE LOVE TO GIVE

What church looked like in our next season was quite different from anything we had experienced. God guided us supernaturally to begin attending a Seattle church - Christian Faith Center (CFC). While leading Kids Co., we would go once a month on a Saturday night to this large church. It was our breath of fresh air and encouragement as we juggled raising a young family, work, and a large ministry.

We would leave on Saturday evening at 5pm for the two-hour drive and arrive at 7pm for the service. After service, the kids changed into their PJs, hopped back in the car and we would drive home, arriving at 11pm. Doing this once a month helped me to stay on course with running the ministry. I had a difficult delivery with Casey, was still recovering after six months, and was ready for a break as a leader. I felt the pull of God to let go of the ministry for a season, and give myself completely to my own children and family.

One evening in August 2000, we did our monthly trek to CFC. There was a special speaker that evening from Wales who spoke from Matthew 14:24 where Jesus was walking on water in the storm and told Peter to get out of the boat and come to Him. At the end of the message the minister asked, "*What boat is Jesus telling you to get out of?*"

Both Clint and I were deeply impacted. It was pretty quiet on the drive home as the kids were asleep and Clint and I were both deep in thought. Finally, we each expressed what we had been feeling and hearing from God . . . we were to stop doing the children's ministry completely and begin coming every Saturday night to CFC. We were both completely in agreement. We both heard God in the same moment, which was not normal for us. Generally, I would hear or 'know' first, then it would take some time for Clint to have the same peace I did. But this time, it was very clear. We talked about what that would look like and how crazy people would think we were. But we both *knew*.

We got things in motion to hand over Kids Co. to other leaders, met with our pastor, and made our exit. When people heard what we were doing, they let us know they didn't understand why we would make the drive every weekend when there were "perfectly good churches in Ellensburg." But we knew this was God's will for us. We found out how important it is to be obedient to the Lord and remain in the center of His will. As the years rolled by, we also found that it not only impacted our own lives, but it had impact on the destinies of many, many lives around us.

For eight years, we attended CFC, driving the two-hour drive there and back weekly to be where we knew God wanted us to be. We always travelled safely across the pass, even in the winter. We knew we were in the center of His will. During that time, God blessed us so abundantly. This large church taught on everything, including finances. One of the mottos of the church was, "We live to give and we love to give." It was something we took to heart. It felt good to say it, believe it, and live it.

GETTING THE PLAN STARTED

We realized eleven years into our marriage that we needed to look seriously at our finances and begin planning for the future. Clint was forty-four, we were self-employed with no plan for retirement, and we had two young kids. I was a stay-at-home, home-schooling mom. I continued in earnest declaring His Word and promises over our lives. I considered that part of my job—that this was a big way I could contribute to my family. But we knew we weren't prepared and hadn't been preparing well for the future. We also knew that simply trying to live on Social Security in our later years wouldn't be nearly enough.

While attending CFC, we were able to attend classes on money management, finishing well, and stewarding increase. We met amazing people who would become our mentors. During this time, God gave us a principle to live by before any wealth came our way. The principle is found in 2 Kings 4:1-7. It is the story of the widow, her sons, and the prophet Elisha. The widow was in debt after her husband passed away and the creditors were coming to take her sons as slaves to pay the debt. Elisha came into the picture and asked her what she had available; what she had in her hand. She had only a small jar of oil. He then told her to have her sons go to neighbors and gather containers - not just a few. When they were all set, Elisha told her to pour the oil into the containers. When the last container was full, the oil stopped and Elisha told the widow to sell the oil, pay the creditors, and live off the rest.

We took this principle and began to set up accounts with the little we had. When our kids were born, Clint's Uncle George and Aunt Thora had given each one $10,000. This was a huge amount to us and we weren't sure what to do with it except we knew that we would save it for them and not spend it on ourselves or anything that we needed as a family. We simply put the money in our local bank in savings accounts for each child. We then took some money we had saved to start some simple retirement accounts of a few thousand dollars each. I also had the $11,000 from my New Mexico Educators Retirement account which had been rolled over into an IRA.

One thing I learned from our Seattle church was something the pastor's wife would often say, 'Earth is short, Heaven is long.' This helped me so much over the years to slow down, not fret or be anxious when difficult times came. I knew I could endure for a short time and keep carrying my hope for the future. I translated this into every area of my life, including financial.

TURN UP THE HEAT CONFERENCE

Another turning point for us came through a children's ministry volunteers conference at CFC. It was called 'Turn Up the Heat,' and we attended as we were volunteering from time to time in the children's ministry. One of the workshops was led by Morgan and Denise, elders in the church. It was all about personal finances and finishing well. That one session was more valuable than pretty much anything else we ever received from that church. Morgan and Denise highly recommended the book, *Smart Couples Finish Rich* by David Bach, to any couple who wanted to see God move in their finances. We immediately bought it.

We both read the book cover to cover and found out so many things we had been doing wrong, so many things we had no clue about concerning finances, and many new ways of thinking. Christian Faith Center was known for the Renewing the Mind message of Romans

12:2, and when we read that book, our minds were well on their way to being renewed, but we still had to walk it out with practical steps and weren't really sure how to do that. We needed a guide.

A couple weeks after the conference, the church bulletin had an announcement for a three-day conference coming up in a couple months. It was to be on financial planning and would have a section pertaining to the book *Smart Couples Finish Rich*. (Bach 2002) We were on it! We signed up immediately and were ready to have our minds further renewed. At the conference, we heard from different speakers and financial advisors. The book had told us we needed a financial advisor if we wanted to do things right and that we needed to interview several to see who might be a good fit for us. We were very nervous as this was something neither of our families had ever done. But we signed up to meet with an advisor through Edward Jones.

The next week, I got a call from one of the Edward Jones financial advisors, Dean, whose office is two hours from where we live. He wanted to come and meet with us. I was stunned and asked him if he knew where we lived. He said yes, and that he traveled all over the U.S. to meet with people he managed accounts for. I set up a meeting for the next Saturday afternoon.

CHOOSING ONE

Interestingly enough, that same week we had a call from a gal, Lisa, with a different company who wanted to meet with us to present her products. We thought, Why not? We were supposed to interview different financial people, something we had never done before, so this would give us our chance. I scheduled her for Friday evening. We had also contacted the insurance rep for our whole life insurance and scheduled that meeting for Saturday morning. We had three meetings in a row and were hoping we were prepared.

The first meeting was fun. Clint and I were given tests to rate how we compared to each other regarding risk taking. When we were finished, we asked Lisa what was our next step. Our desire was to have help with investing what little amount we did have. She opened up her folder and began showing us more tests, but these cost from $400 to $1,600 per test! We were shocked, signed up for nothing, and thanked Lisa for coming.

The next morning, we met with the insurance guy. The *Smart Couples Finish Rich* book had said this type of meeting would be the most difficult one we would have. Trying to drop whole life insurance to move to term life was the smartest thing to do, but it was something insurance sales people really didn't like. We needed to be prepared to encounter some possible rudeness in trying to make the switch because whole life policies were the bread and butter of insurance agents. We were interested to see if this would really happen. Sure enough, the minute we brought up what we wanted to do, we got tremendous push back including being accused of not loving our children because the whole life policy contained a savings element. It was assumed that we would not continue saving for our future without the whole life type of policy. We stuck to our guns, though, and eventually got the agent to make the changes we wanted.

An hour later, Dean from Edward Jones showed up. We had our list of questions, the first being how much will this cost us? When we heard it would cost us nothing to have Dean as our financial adviser, that his job was to help us save and increase our money, we were amazed. He told us that initially he would put our money into mutual fund accounts with very low fees attached. He would eventually make his money when we had enough to move to stock accounts. We found we really enjoyed visiting with Dean. He explained the changes he would make in all our accounts and how he would invest our money to keep it growing. We chose Dean.

I also chose Dean for my dad's accounts as he had limited funds, was in his early eighties, and needed his accounts to be managed well to stretch into whatever the future might bring. My dad loved Dean, and even though he had never had a financial advisor in his life, he handled this new experience well. In the end, it was a brilliant choice as dad's accounts increased significantly because of the wonder of compound interest and proper managing by Dean. The money covered him well through the end of his life.

As we worked with Dean, we saw that setting up our accounts into different savings 'containers' had been smart. Dean helped us tweak the accounts and make decisions as to how much we wanted to fund our kids' college accounts and what types of retirement accounts to open as we were self-employed. From that point on, I did everything I could to save money to drop into the non-retirement accounts. I had yard sales, selling everything I could think of. The kids helped me set up a road-side table to sell vegetables and lemonade in the summer. I tweaked the grocery spending to the bare minimum while still eating healthy. Every little bit extra I dropped into those accounts. I was determined to finish well and see those accounts fill up.

DR. INCREASE

A special speaker named Bob Harrison came to our Seattle church and spoke about Kingdom increase, innovative success strategies in business, and the wisdom of God in the financial areas of our lives. He spoke from a business perspective and gave practical steps to begin to walk in abundance out of our connection with God. It really spoke to me, and I began putting many of the practical steps into place. We soon heard that he had a series of meetings in Portland, Oregon. Since Clint's sister lived in that area, we planned a trip to visit her and attend one of the meetings.

There were around seven hundred people at the meeting. Bob shared many of the principles he had learned throughout the years. He didn't just teach about money. He talked about changing mindsets and core beliefs so people could live overcoming and victorious lives: physically, spiritually, and in personal relationships. He said something that resonated so strongly with me. He said, "*I am going to give you a key to abundance. In this room of 700 or so people, only 3% will do what I am about to tell you to do.*" Immediately, I said in my head, '*I will be one of the 3%.*'

He said, "Say this every day for a year: *The Lord is increasing us more and more, us and our children. We are blessed of the Lord who made heaven and earth.*" I turned to Clint and said, '*I will be one of the 3%.*' And I was. I said that verse (Psalm 115:14-15) every day, multiple times a day for that whole year, and I continue to say it at least weekly. It was a good vow to make!

Eighteen years later, we are walking in the fruit of that verse. He *has* increased us more and more, us and our children. We *are* blessed of the Lord who made Heaven and earth.

As we were believing and declaring, we also began to *do* the Word. There was a young couple in our Seattle church who were struggling to make their monthly house payment. God put on our hearts to begin giving them $250 a month toward their mortgage. It was certainly an extravagant amount for us, but so worth the results in our hearts and the joy and relief it brought to them. Our hope was that as we gave, there would come a time in this young couple's life that they would "pay it forward" to do the same for someone else. We don't know if that has happened, as they moved on as did we, but knowing God and how He works signs and wonders into our lives, it probably has!

$90,000 IN THREE YEARS

During these years, CFC was experiencing great growth. It was evident that God was blessing this church and we were so grateful to be a part of it. The church began to look at expanding. They needed a larger campus than the one we had been attending. Soon they found an adequate piece of land and began a fund-raising campaign. We attended a special dinner where we were asked to pledge any amount to give that we felt the Lord tell us for the next three years. We had some time to pray and talk together after the meal. I tend to be more of a risk-taker where giving is concerned and I set my sights on $100,000, a seemingly impossible amount. Clint wasn't so sure and he suggested $80,000, also a seemingly impossible amount. We eventually settled on $90,000. Then it was a matter of hearing from God, giving consistently, and walking it out.

Slowly but surely, we whittled away at that $90,000 pledge as if it was a debt we owed. We took seriously the verses in Psalm 15:4 (NKJV) about the righteous man: "… *he who swears to his own hurt and does not change,*" and Ecclesiastes 5:4 (NASB) "*When you make a vow to God, do not be late in paying it; for He takes no delight in fools. Pay what you vow!*"

We divided the pledge into three $30,000 chunks to pay over the three years and began setting aside money toward that. It was remarkable how Clint would get an extra job so we would have more, or I would think of something we could sell, or someone would just give us money. Every year, we chipped away at that pledge until it was completely done.

At the time, we were meeting in a once-a-month home group with some families in Seattle. In one of our home group meetings toward the end of the three-year pledge period, we all began talking about the pledge. We had just paid our portion off and shared that. The leaders were amazed. They said we were in the top 10% then because they knew for a fact that 90% of the people never finished or planned to finish their pledges. We were amazed to find out how few people actually fulfilled their giving commitment. Our friends were amazed to find that we had.

This was another lesson on the journey where God was showing us how important character and integrity is. We may not have been the most gifted or talented or vocal or even noticed in the church, but like Cornelius in Acts 10, we were noticed by heaven. We knew that the favor of God was on us, not only because we declared His promises over us, but because we were also doers of the Word and not just hearers (James 1:22).

TAKING THE STEPS

Throughout this time, I began to have a desire to increase our giving from being $10 givers to eventually giving millions. I had routinely given $10 for birthday gifts or special offerings. I had begun to take a bit of cash with me to have available to give if I felt God highlighting someone to give to. But I was feeling the nudge to up the amount that I believed I was capable of giving. I began to take risk, step out, and give $20 bills away.

But I had a dream. I wanted to keep increasing our giving level. I put my dream into words in my declarations:

1. We are seeing our businesses increase and expand, bringing in hundreds of thousands and millions of dollars to the Kingdom.

2. Where once we gave $10, now we give hundreds.

3. Where once we gave $10, now we give thousands.

4. Where once we gave $10, now we give ten-thousands.

5. Where once we gave $10, now we give hundred-thousands.

6. Where once we gave $10, now we give millions. Amen!

7. We are giving 90% of our income and living quite well (with houses and lands and much increase) on the 10%.

I remember so many of the steps along to way to bigger and bigger giving. I began with giving $1 a week in my church in Albuquerque.

Then when I got my teaching job, I was able to increase my giving level to be a $10 giver. After I got married, we were able to be $20 givers. Whenever our kids were invited to birthday parties, we would buy $20 gifts or just give cash. It was fun seeing the amazement and delight on the faces of the receivers–that amount seemed so extravagant to them.

The next goal was to become $50 givers. Fortunately, friends' birthdays were spaced out over the year, so this wasn't too difficult to do. I remember at the $50 giving amount people were stunned. It was so unusual for them to have someone give $50 for even a birthday present that they didn't really know what to do with that. Each time I tucked a $50 bill into a card, I knew I was stretching my faith and planting a seed. I knew eventually the harvest would come.

Graduations proved to be the catalyst to become $100 givers. I usually had a stash of cash that I could draw from for the next opportunity to give. It felt so good to be able to pull out that crisp $100 bill to put in the card for a struggling student.

It took a bit longer to reach the $1,000 giver level, but we did it. There were strategic points where we knew it was time to give $1,000. So we did. Not every gift during that season would be at that level, but many were. We would continue giving at the $20, $50, and $100 level as we stretched ourselves further and further in our giving. God always provided seed to the sower and gave us back an abundant supply (2 Corinthians 9:10).

I also read about a couple who had bought a ranch in eastern Oregon in 1991 for $3.6 million. After attempting to run the ranch for profit and that venture failing, they eventually donated the entire

ranch in 1996 to Young Life–a ministry for teens. Young Life has operated this Washington Family Ranch as a summer Young Life camp
since then, and it has become an amazing place where teens encounter
God. I cut the article about it from the magazine and pinned it above
my desk. I told Clint this was my dream–to have millions of dollars someday to pour into the Kingdom. I began to dream of what it
would be like to have the ability to do that kind of extravagant giving.

Meanwhile, God was teaching me to listen to His voice even in
my giving, to be obedient to Him and hear when He said Yes, and
when He said No.

CON MAN AT THE GAS STATION

Over the eight years we attended CFC, we developed many friendships. There were lots of homeschoolers who went to the church. We
became part of that community. As a result, the kids and I would go
over to Seattle in the middle of the week from time to time for group
science classes, zoo visits, and homeschool activities. We loved it all!

One afternoon, we were returning from Seattle. Upon getting
into Ellensburg, I realized I needed gas, so I stopped at a station near
the West Interchange, hopped out of the car, and began to fill up. A
man approached me on foot, and I instantly got the feeling of being
slimed. The man asked me for $20 because he needed to buy a part
for his car which had broken down on the freeway. I told him I didn't
have any cash on me. I was on high alert at this point, and I thought
back to the portion of the freeway he said he was stranded on that
I had just driven past. I hadn't seen any stranded car. The man said

some wonderful people had picked him up and brought him into town to get the part for his car.

A very nice white Cadillac Escalade pulled up with a woman driving and a man in the back seat behind her. I felt the same slimy feeling from these people. I "saw" a kind of dirty cloud surrounding them, as well. The man talking to me told me that he would give me the Christian CDs he had in his car if I would just give him $20. Again, I told him I didn't have any cash. I asked if perhaps he could purchase the car part he needed at the gas station store. I was thinking I could be compassionate and at least go and buy him this $20 part with my debit card. I was sorting through confusion in my mind as to what God would have me do. I should have a heart of compassion for those in need, for the poor (he did look kind of shabby), but at the same time I had all these red warning lights flashing in my brain. I was desperately seeking the mind of God as I spoke with the man. He said the gas station store didn't have the part he needed. Cash would be best.

Then I had the thought that I could meet him at an auto parts store in town and buy him the part there. I asked him if he knew where the store was that I had in mind. He and the lady driving the Escalade said they did. I asked them if they would meet me there and they said yes. He then got in the vehicle and they drove away. But they drove in the opposite direction of the auto parts store. I finished pumping the gas and drove to the store. I didn't see their vehicle, so I went inside and asked if these people had shown up. The guys in the store got a look on their faces and said they knew of this group of people. They had been in and around town scamming people from time to time over the past several years. And then I knew. Because of the voice of the Holy Spirit in my heart, even though my mind was trying to figure it out and I felt confusion, I had followed His lead and I had prospered. I was so thankful. I was also mad, so I went directly to the police station and reported the people, the vehicle they were in, and what they had tried to do.

Two days later, I was telling a friend about how listening to those quiet impressions of the Holy Spirit had spared me even wasting $20 and being scammed. She then told me she had been at a grocery store the day before loading her groceries into her car, and a gentleman had approached her and asked for $20. Her two teenage kids in the car begged her not to give the man any money because they could feel that he was scamming their mom. She was so tenderhearted and felt pushed into giving him something, so she handed him $20. She said as he left (in the white Escalade), she felt this nasty slime all over her and she knew she had been manipulated and lied to. It took her several days to get over the bad feeling she had been left with.

Through times like these, where I heard God's voice and responded, I was learning that prosperity is not only resources and finances, but protection, as well. There have been so many times in my life I have been protected from accidents, from wrong relationships, from others' hidden agendas, and much more. Once again, I was so grateful for the leading of the Holy Spirit, that I hear His voice consistently, and that His plans for me have always been, and are, only good. I was growing in my ability to hear God's voice over finances–even the very small amount of $20. 3 John 1:2 (KJV) began to mean so much more, "*Beloved, I wish above all things that you may prosper and be in health, even as your soul prospers.*"

JENNIFER

One of the most inspiring people in my life during this season was Jennifer. Both of us were homeschool moms with kids in the same age range. She and her husband were starting a new business in town and were prospering abundantly. Jennifer was fierce in believing God for finances and increase. She had such a determination about her that creative ideas for increase would come constantly. She also was fierce in her declarations. She would take forty minutes each day to speak God's promises over her family. Both our families were traveling the four-hour round trip each weekend for "Seattle church," and we were receiving the same inspiring messages. The thing about Jennifer was that she was taking what she heard and doing it. She was not only a hearer of the Word; she was also a doer. I admired that.

Watching her example caused me to grow in my faith and increase what I had already been doing. Prior to this, I had been declaring and believing, but not at the level I wanted to. Jennifer inspired me and I began speaking my eleven pages of declarations out loud daily. I even recorded them on cassette tapes and digitally with my computer, and played them back as I washed dishes, did laundry, made dinner, or did art projects with the kids. I wanted the Word going in me constantly, in season and out, not just when it was convenient. God's Word began to flow out of me consistently. I leveled up and began to speak like Moses told Joshua in Joshua 1:8 (NASB), "*This book of the law shall not depart from your mouth, but you shall meditate on it day and night, so that you may be careful to do according to all that is written in it; for then you will make your way prosperous, and then you will achieve success."* I am so grateful for Jennifer and the inspiration she was to me to get back on track.

INCREASED DECLARATIONS

My eleven pages of declarations covered every possible thing in our lives. They covered our health, our relationships, our wealth and increase, our animals and livestock, our desire for the Word and my own personal commitment, faith, confidence, identity, and giving. There were large portions of scripture as well. These were the promises of God to me and my family. Like Joshua said in Joshua 24:15b (NKJV), *"But as for me and my house, we will serve the Lord."*

As a result of the increase in declaring His Word, I began hearing Jesus more on who to give to, how much to give and when to give. He said in John 15:7 that if I abide in Him and His words abide in me, I will ask what I will and it will be granted to me. I was daily abiding in His Word through this avenue of declaring scripture after scripture, promise after promise over our lives. Our giving greatly increased as a result. We gave groceries, clothing, gift cards, computers, and cash. Whenever we saw a need, we asked God what we were to do and then we took steps to meet the need. We lived with an open hand.

I was learning to walk by faith, not by sight (2 Corinthians 5:7), to release the seemingly impossible through my words mixed with my faith–all given by my Father God. This was another step on the road to abundance as I kept building momentum in the spirit realm.

EXTRAVAGANT GIVING

Another great gift to me from Jennifer was her introduction to the teaching of Robert Morris, the pastor of Gateway Church near Fort Worth, Texas. He had taught a series on giving called "*The Blessed Life.*" Jennifer gave me the entire series on video tape to watch. He talked about extravagant, over-the-top generosity. It lit a fire in me like nothing else had ever done. His testimony of giving away everything resonated so deeply in me . . . how God had challenged him to give a very large, extravagant offering–house, all bank accounts, cars, everything. He had been in his quiet time with the Lord and thinking about how God gave everything in Jesus. He felt like the Lord asked him, '*Would you give everything?*' His response was, *Yes!* With his wife on board, they walked out the plan God had given them to give it all away. As they set aside the amount to give, the cars to give, and the house, God provided them with the next thing in their lives so they weren't left homeless and destitute for any amount of time. But they gave it all.

I so wanted to do this and approached Clint with the possibilities. At that time, Kelcy was taking ballet classes through a local dance studio. Amy, the young gal who ran the studio, was under pressure to buy the building her studio was in or lose it, and my heart went out to her. I wanted to give everything in our retirement accounts (which would have been just enough) to pay off her mortgage. It was extravagant, it was big, and it didn't happen. Clint was not ready for that big of a leap into the world of extravagant giving. Instead, he was willing to give $5,000 towards the Christmas show she needed funding for, and that in itself was quite large, quite extravagant considering our income and financial ability. It was the next step for us.

We realized that this type of giving was sacrificial. We had to adjust what we wanted to do with that money, which many times meant deferring upgrading our lifestyle, keeping a worn out couch a bit longer, or driving an older car for a few more years, but we wanted to keep giving fresh in our hearts. We wanted our lives to be turned outward. We wanted to give as the Lord said to give, not grudgingly or out of compulsion (2 Corinthians 9:7) and watch the changes in our hearts. We would obey whenever God said. We were glad to do it. It was exciting.

It did take a while for Clint and me to get on the same page where giving was concerned. We had both been raised in families who tithed to the church and we understood how important it was to give the 10%, but neither of us had been taught about offerings and living with a constant outward flow. I was willing to give the farm away the minute I discovered the joy of extravagant generosity, but Clint wasn't. We had many discussions on what that type of giving should look like. I had a much greater desire to give than he did.

Eventually we settled on a way that worked for both of us. Every time we would receive any money, we would set aside the tithe and an amount over and above the tithe. I would take this in cash and put it in an envelope that was my "giving cash." Then I had the freedom to give whenever and to whomever I felt God telling me to give. Clint was comfortable with this plan and felt safe, and I had enough free-dom to give as I felt God leading me. It worked out great. There were times from that point on that we would stretch even further to give.

CARS AND BETTER CARS

A huge blessing for both Clint and me was that we had similar economic upbringings. We were both uncomfortable with any kind of debt, so we just didn't go there. We did have credit cards and still do. We have both been wise in using those credit cards as tools and never carrying a balance, always paying it off every month. If anything, Clint is more conservative financially than I am, but we both agreed on the big things.

One of those big things was buying vehicles. I only once bought a brand new off-the-lot car. I was single and gave that kind of debt a try. I hated it, and by the time I met Clint, the car had been sold, and I had no debt. Throughout our marriage, we only bought used cars. God always brought us good deals. I would have liked bigger and better cars, but I was satisfied with what we had. For us, our cars were not status symbols, so we were willing to do with less and drive them longer than the average family.

The first car we bought together was a used Nissan Sentra. It was a great little car and I loved it. Clint always had his work truck, so the little car was mine. But as our family grew, we needed a bigger car. It was difficult to navigate a baby car seat in the back with a two-door car. We sold the Nissan to a private party and found a used Chevy Impala with low mileage for a great price. I found I really liked the Impala because it was just big enough and had a huge trunk space. I was satisfied with that car and we drove it all the way up to 220,000 miles. It was the car we took back and forth to Seattle every weekend for the eight years we were involved at CFC. The car finally got to the point where to keep it running safely, we would need to put more money into it than it was worth, so we began looking for another car. Because the Impala had worked so well for us, that was what we had our eye on.

As we were going back and forth to Seattle often, we looked for cars in that area, which had more options than our smaller town. By now the internet was a great way to do research, and Clint found a used Impala in Bellevue (close to Seattle) that looked perfect. On our next trip over, we stopped by the dealer to look at the car. It was unusual because this used Chevy Impala was at a Saturn dealership. The car wasn't available to purchase that day, so we decided that the kids and I would stop by in the middle of the week when I had another trip over planned.

We had a set $10,000 cash price limit with our car as a trade-in. This newer Impala was being offered at over $13,000. When I stopped by later in the week, the sales people did their thing and tried to get me to move on my price. I was honest and told them we had $10,000 cash and that was it. I was very firm on that price and willing to walk if I couldn't get the car for that with our trade-in. After about thirty minutes of meeting with the first guy who had no success in getting me to change my mind, his manager came in and began working me over. He told me I didn't care about the safety of my kids, among other things. I began to see red. Anyone who knows me knows that when I set my feet, I will not be moved. The more someone pushes, the more I will resist. I was so angry that he told me I didn't love my kids because I wouldn't buy his car at his price that I got up and left. I was so mad, I had to pray the whole two-hour trip home!

A couple days later, the boss called and talked to Clint. He tried to get him to buy the car for the price the dealer wanted. But at that point, we were done so we just said no. We told each other that if God wanted us to have that car, He would make a way and the car could not be sold to anyone else. Then we just forgot about it.

About a month later, we were vacationing with friends in their place in Idaho and my cell phone rang. It was an unknown number, but I answered it. It was the manager from the dealership. He said he had that very Impala and he wanted to offer it to us for $9,000. I laughed inside and wondered if he knew who I was, the lady he wouldn't sell the exact same car to for $10,000 a month before. I felt that justice was done!

Clint took over the call and said we would take the car for the $9,000 if we could put it on our credit card. The manager said that was absolutely fine. We said we were out of town and wouldn't be able to pick it up and pay for it until the next Sunday. He was fine with that and said he would have his finance person there to complete the transaction.

The next Sunday, we arrived at the dealership ready to complete the sale. When we pulled out our credit card to pay, the finance person said that it would not be possible for us to pay with a credit card. We told him what his manager had told us and that it would be no big deal for us to walk away again. He shrugged and said okay, and that the credit card fee would be paid by the boss since he had made the deal with us. We turned in our old Impala and drove away in the car God had made the arrangements for. The blessing of the Lord makes rich and adds no sorrow with it!

JOSEPH

Several years later, there was an interesting twist on our car story which involved one of our international students, Joseph. Joseph was from China and lived with us for three years while he was attending Central Washington University here in Ellensburg. He was nineteen and ready to buy his first car. His father was funding him and told him he had up to $19,000 to spend. Joseph asked us to go to Seattle with him to look for cars. We found that our Chinese students (in fact, pretty much all of our international student friends) were nicely well off, most of them well-funded by their parents. Just the fact that they were able to attend universities in the United States meant they were probably in the top 10% wealth-wise of their nations. Joseph was doing pretty well.

Another thing we found in hosting international students is that status symbols are very important, especially to the Chinese. The brand is more important than the product, and Joseph wanted a BMW, Mercedes, Cadillac, or an Audi. He was going high end. As we had never looked at those types of cars, we really didn't know what dealerships to go to for used cars in that class. The car-buying trip was scheduled for the next Saturday. I suddenly remembered the Saturn dealership where we had bought our current used Impala. I had a strong impression that we should go there first. Joseph had been looking up places with the types of cars he wanted and he had several places he wanted to look at as well.

Our first stop was the Saturn dealership, except it was no longer a Saturn dealership. Apparently, the Saturn Corporation had gone bankrupt in 2010 and the dealership no longer existed. It was now a used car dealership for luxury cars. The lot was filled with used BMWs, Mercedes, Cadillacs, and Audis! The costs of these cars were still high, but Joseph found a very nice Audi for $19,000. I knew that God had most definitely led us here and that it had not just been a random thought that had popped into my head. It had been His voice leading us. But Joseph wasn't as sure and he wanted to look at another car in a lot forty-five minutes away. We went ahead and took him, but that car was a bust. We ended up back at the first one. One thing I learned from this adventure is that when God prompts, it is always the best way. We wasted an hour and a half driving, frustrated with big city traffic and exhausted, simply because Joseph didn't trust the leading of the Lord. I realized that I was hearing Him well at this point in my life, and I could trust the inner voice, inner impressions, and His goodness in bringing favor and blessing into our lives.

Joseph did purchase that $19,000 Audi, and it served him well for his remaining time in Ellensburg.

Our most recent car purchase was very similar to Joseph's car purchase. We knew we needed another car soon as there were 220,000 plus miles on our miracle Impala. Neither of us like the whole car selling and buying thing, but Clint began looking online for Impalas again. He hadn't seen anything he liked.

One day I had the sense that we should look at a local dealership (one we didn't particularly like but the impression was pretty strong). We went to the dealership and there was our next Impala. It had been sitting on their lot for ten months. They just couldn't seem to flip it and the price kept dropping and dropping. The thing about this car that brought me great joy and let me know the great, great love of God for me was that it had leather interior, a leather steering wheel cover, heated seats, and many more wonderful things that I had specifically wanted. Yay God!

Again, it was the Lord who led us, the Lord who guided us, and the Lord who brought the blessing and increase into our lives. I have seen that every car we have bought has had the favor and direction of God on it. He has led us into buying the next car every time. It is a fun adventure to live a life in friendship and relationship with Him!

JUST BEFORE

Clint's Uncle George and Aunt Thora had lived a good life. They were conservative in politics and religion. They loved God and people but never had any children. Clint and his three sisters filled that role. While growing up, they would visit Uncle George and Aunt Thora for a couple weeks every summer at their home on a small lake in Woodland, Washington. George and Thora would take care of them well with camping trips, ice skating shows, trips to the beach, theater shows, Lipizzaner horse shows, and more.

Uncle George had been the school superintendent in Woodland and Thora had been a school teacher throughout her career. They were now retired, well advanced in age and doing well, living quite frugally in their simple house on the lake. The town was a bedroom community of Portland, about half an hour north of the Vancouver/Portland area, but was pretty laid back without much growth. Eventually, Uncle George realized that he could no longer keep up with home ownership, and he decided they would move into the local residential retirement center.

One day, I had the thought that Clint must call Uncle George and ask him about his house, what was his plan for it, and could we possibly buy it. George was so glad Clint called because he had just been discussing the possible sale of the house to one of his neighbors. The lady had offered him at least $20,000 under market and he was about to say yes. In fact, he was meeting with the lady the next day to solidify the sale.

When Clint called, George was happy to gift it to his nieces and nephew. Through the weeks that followed, it was decided that the house would be gifted to Clint's older unmarried sister as her inheritance would eventually go to the other three siblings. In Clint's family, I saw fairness with no greed played out. It was an amazing thing to me. I found it honoring and something I wanted to continue with our kids. So the transaction occurred, and everyone was satisfied with the results. This was one of our first 'just before' moments where God intervened in our plans through an idea or a nudge in order to bring us into a place of blessing.

Uncle George passed away a few years after and Thora continued to live at the retirement facility, although they moved her to the medical side after George passed. Within a few weeks of George's death, Clint's sister contacted me and asked me to take all his account information and put it in the QuickBooks accounting software program, as I was familiar with it. This would make things easier for her as the personal representative of his Trust. When I saw the amount of wealth that George and Thora had amassed and managed well, I was blown away. George left a legacy for his nephew and nieces. I was personally inspired by how he managed his money and his life. It gave me a vision and permission to go after the same for Clint and me. He was an administrator extraordinaire! He had left a sealed envelope for Clint's sister to open at his death giving instructions, phone numbers, important people to connect with, numbers and places of all his accounts, and even his own obituary. It made closure so easy upon his death. I wanted to leave that kind of legacy and blessing for my own kids.

Generally, when a spouse in a marriage of longevity passes away, the other spouse soon follows, but this was not the case with Thora. George and Thora were married in 1946 and had fifty-seven years of a good marriage. George passed away in March of 2003, but Thora kept hanging on. We all wondered why she was lingering and when it would be her time. She had severe dementia and didn't know any of us, although we all continued to visit her as regularly as we could. Then on November 30, 2004, she passed away.

Clint's sister began the process of closing things down once Thora passed in late 2004. Within two weeks, we had a check deposited into our bank account that represented a full quarter of their estate. Then we found out the amazing thing. When George gifted the house to Clint's sister, because it was a gift and not a sale, a certain amount of time needed to pass before the estate was closed in order keep the house value from being added to the estate. Thora passed away three days after that date. This meant that the value of the house was not added to the entire estate, potentially putting the estate value over the non-taxable inheritance amount. If she had passed away any time before that look-back date, there would have been a large state tax on the entire estate. Instead, because God had Thora wait a few more months beyond George's death, even to the point of a three-day difference, there was would be no tax at all on the estate and it was split out within two weeks.

The house is still in the family and has increased four times in value as the market in the area has exploded. It was such a great investment and a God-moment when we knew to call George and let him know our interest in purchasing the house. It has become very clear to us that God is interested in our finances and in increasing us. 2 Chronicles 16:9 says *"For the eyes of the LORD move to and fro throughout the earth that He may strongly support those whose heart is completely His"* (NASB). I know that He knows He can trust us, and when He impresses us to give, we will give. We will not hold back. Because of this, His increase has come and has continued. We walk in the favor of the Lord because He can trust us to do what He prompts us to do. It is a wonderful way to live!

Chapter 5

TALK TIME, INTERNATIONAL STUDENTS & FALL PARTIES

We interacted with international students at CWU on many levels, from hosting fall apple cider-making parties and Farm Days, having cooking classes at our house, taking students shopping at Costco, visiting popular tourist towns like Leavenworth, Washington, to having a few live with us while they were here in college. Eventually we branched out from the AUAP program with only Japanese students and added in the whole international student program from the university. Now we had many nations coming and going from our home—Saudi Arabians, Chinese, Taiwanese, French, Mexican, Scottish, and many more.

There was a weekly meeting on campus called Talk Time which our family joined. Here international full-time, part-time and transfer students could come to practice their English with Americans. There were usually fifteen to twenty students who came weekly. We were divided up at tables of six to eight with one English speaker and five or more international students. There was an ice breaker, then a short ten-minute lesson on topics such as Valentine's Day, anxiety around finals and tests, cultural differences in governments, traits of a leader, family celebrations, and more. We were given a series of questions to discuss around our table group for twenty minutes or so. We met many students from all over the world. Our family would go weekly. We all developed great listening and leadership skills. Even our kids learned how to make people from other cultures with different languages feel comfortable and loved.

At our Talk Time table groups, we would get to know students and invite those who God highlighted to come to our home for a meal, to ride a horse, visit a farm, play games, and enjoy American family life. These students enriched our lives so much. It was another way to take giving to a new level. Opening up our home from only the Japanese AUAP student groups to all the international students at the university gave us many more students to care for.

From this group, we began hosting larger fall apple cider-making parties. Soon we had the university advisors bringing students out to our place by the vanload as we continued the party for six hours in two-hour shifts to give everyone the farm experience. One year, we had over two hundred students descend on the farm. We were completely exhausted at the end of the day. After that, we were all in agreement that smaller groups were much better and scaled back considerably.

Because of the needs of the students, we started a new ministry called The Storehouse. International students would stay at the university for varying lengths of time. Some were here for only three months, some for six months, some for a full year, and some for their entire college experience of four years or more. We began to see a need with the outgoing international students. They would come with only a suitcase and would need to buy furniture, bedding, and kitchen items to furnish some of the dorms they were housed in. Sometimes they needed rides to the stores or Goodwill to pick up new and used items. At the end of their stays, they needed a place to dispose of or take the items. We found that many students just threw away almost brand-new microwaves, furniture, and household items into the college dumpsters. Our idea was to take a trailer down to the dorms, pick up these items, sort and store them in our shop, and when the next load of students arrived, let them "shop" for these free things. We worked with the university to provide this service, and it worked so well that we kept it going for several years.

CHRISTMAS AT CFC

Our Seattle church always put on an amazing Christmas production where Jesus was presented in splendor and awe. I got to thinking how it would be so cool to be able to take a group of international Talk Time students over to Seattle for one of these special services. We presented the idea at Talk Time and many students were interested. By the time we finished the sign-ups, we had forty-eight people who wanted to go. My dream was to rent a big Greyhound-type bus to show that we honored these students and wanted to bless them with the best. In researching, I found that a bus the size we would need would run around $1,000 for such a trip. Even though that was a huge amount for us at the time, we had money in our giving account, so we went for it.

What an amazing trip! We packed into the bus, left early, and had a blast all the way over to Seattle, even stopping at the mall so everyone could have a bit of shopping time and get something to eat. What we didn't count on was the ice storm that hit Seattle that day. Our time at the mall was cut short because of the poor driving conditions, but we went ahead and pressed on to the church. On one of the steep Seattle hills, our bus simply could not make it up. We would get half-way up, then begin sliding down backwards. It was quite an adventure!

Eventually, we arrived at the church just a few minutes before the program was to begin. I had arranged with one of the pastors to have a section roped off for fifty people, and they were excited for us to come. Our bus pulled in, the students piled out, and we found we had no seats. One of the ushers had removed the ropes sectioning off our reserved section and had let others sit there. I was so mad! Not one of my best moments. But God used it to teach me something about who He had made me to be.

Our students had to be seated in a side wing which wasn't optimal. The program was to start and the production seemed to be experiencing a major glitch. They couldn't get the power connected in the way they needed, so everything was on hold. I was still angry and felt I couldn't just sit and wait, so I got up to be alone at the back of the sanctuary. I was standing behind the sound board and watching multiple people working furiously to fix whatever the problem was.

As I stood there, I heard Holy Spirit say, *"You know this is happening because of you, don't you?"* I instantly realized that my tremendous anger was affecting the atmosphere so much that it was causing electrical disturbances in the church's system. I released all the pent-up emotion quickly and repented. Within thirty seconds, everything was fine and the program started. It was full of faith and the promise of God. Many of our students who had never heard the gospel were introduced to Jesus in a beautiful and profound way that night.

This was also such a lesson in how much each of us affects the spirit realm around us, how we can shift the atmosphere in a place by our very thoughts or our attitude when we walk into a room. What we are carrying, thinking, and bringing to that situation will have impact. I was beginning to see that even though I was not out evangelizing anybody, I was definitely impacting the world around me. I was so thankful for that lesson. I was growing in God as a stay-at-home mom and lover of Jesus and His people all over the world—all from my own backyard. Jesus was bringing the people to me! I needed to be vigilant to steward this responsibility well.

ENTER BETHEL

It was the beginning of 2009. One of the pastors of our Seattle church mentioned she had taken her daughters to a two-week summer worship school the previous summer at a church called Bethel in Redding, California. She mentioned that as the children were worshiping in the sanctuary, a lady who was deaf in one ear walked past the open door and was instantly healed of her deafness. I loved this testimony of healing and I wanted to be in a place where the presence of God was so large that someone walking through the church would receive healing or whatever else they needed from Him. I also wanted to make that same atmosphere of seeking and hearing from God available to my own kids, Kelcy and Casey.

I began looking into this church and worship school. I found that Kelcy, who was now thirteen, was too old to attend the children's school, but she could attend the adult school. Since I didn't know much about the church and the leadership, I decided to apply as well. Both of us were accepted and I found housing for the three and a half weeks we would be in Redding for the worship school.

We arrived in late June to one hundred plus degree heat. Although that was unpleasant and somewhat of a shock, the worship that came out of this church, the worship leaders from around the world who came as instructors, and the presence of God in the place made everything worth it. Casey had stayed home with Clint as he was too young for the adult school and we thought that this trip would be a one-time deal. But three days in, I was rocked with the nearness of God, with His anointing, goodness, presence, and love. I couldn't get enough and my heart was completely opened. I HAD to go back. I had to keep coming and bring my whole family into this deep, deep awareness of God and His heart for us.

At the end of our three and a half weeks, as we drove away from that amazing place that first summer of 2009, I cried out to God to please let me come back, to please make a way for us to experience Him in that way more and more. What a time in God we had had.

What an opening up of things in me and of reconnecting to His divine purpose and plan for my life. I was forever grateful. That summer, I heard God say to me that He was redeeming my years from ages thirteen to nineteen in New Mexico when I was introduced to the discerning of spirits gifting. It had brought such fear and confusion upon me as I had no one to teach me how to use it. Now, through Bethel and these people emphasizing His presence and connection with His heart, I was being taught and my heart was healing.

When I got home, I was a different person. I had spent the past thirteen years rightly focusing on my family, on raising Godly kids and giving my everything to ministry. Now there was a shift. Worship became front and center in my heart, and all I wanted to do was spend time worshipping Him and encountering His presence. Every day, I would go out to our shop where we had a large second story bonus-room space. We weren't using the space for homeschooling any longer, so I set up a keyboard and began printing out worship songs and connecting with God for several hours at a time. It became my 'house of prayer.' I had found that I did not have to wait for God to come to me for those amazing moments of encounter to happen randomly, but I could pursue God, feel His presence, hear His voice, and be encompassed and encountered by Him whenever I wanted. It was a revelation, and I was so grateful.

WORSHIP NIGHTS

My world had shifted dramatically in my pursuit of God, and I asked my family to join with me for a family worship night one night a week. We began on Friday nights for thirty minutes to an hour of worshipping together in our living room. It was a highlight of my week, and I was so glad my family wanted to share it together with me.

One Friday night, the university was going into Spring Break, so we invited a sweet Japanese student, Eri, to have dinner with us as she was not traveling and was alone in her dorm. After we ate and visited, I told her that Friday night was our family night to worship together and asked if she would like to join us. She said she definitely would.

Eri had come to America without knowing God. While on campus one day, an American student had walked up to her and asked her if she knew Jesus. Eri said no, but she was interested. Out of that conversation and new relationship, she accepted Jesus. She was a brand-new Christian when we met her and carried such a tender and pure heart.

We worshiped together that Friday night and when we finished, we asked Eri if she thought having a weekly worship night might be something other international students would enjoy. She gave a resounding yes, and suggested that Friday nights would be the best night of the week for something like this. That was the beginning of Friday Worship Nights at our house.

The next week, Eri invited four other Japanese girls. We picked them up from the university and brought them to our house. We live seven miles from the university and very few of the international students have cars or driver's licenses in the United States. Many of them have never even driven in their home countries, so we had to figure out a way to get students to and from the university. By the third

Worship Night, we had fifteen students show up. We recruited some American friends and other American students with cars who also wanted to join in with our weekly dinner and worship times. Soon we had several full cars making the trek from CWU to our house.

Over the years, Worship Nights were an amazing time of connecting Jesus and His heart with the nations who were at our doorstep. Our house was filled with students from China, Hong Kong, South Korea, Taiwan, Japan, Saudi Arabia, Mexico, and more. God gave us two amazing girls from Hong Kong, Sam and Monica, who would come an hour or two early on Friday and prepare lots of food. I could concentrate on the spiritual focus of the night while they took care of the practical. I would give them money every week to go and purchase the food and supplies they would need to cook. Monica was a nutrition major at the university, so we always had the best meals!

On Friday night, we would gather together, eat and visit in our house, then go upstairs to our shop bonus-room for worship and ministry. We had decorated the space beautifully with flags of the world, worship lighting, instruments, comfy couches and chairs, mattresses, blankets and pillows around on the floor, supplies for artwork, song books for singing, and love in our hearts. This weekly group would grow from twenty to fifty depending on how much homework and studying for tests students had to do that particular week. We saw salvations, God touching everyone on very deep levels, and even a couple baptisms in our home's small swimming pool. These were awesome times and made a deep impact on many lives, including our own and the "team" of Americans God had raised up to serve beside us.

OBED-EDOM

There is a story in I Chronicles 13:13-14 about Obed-Edom, who ended up having the ark of the covenant at his house for three months after it was returned from the Philistines who had stolen it. King David was bringing the ark back to Jerusalem. On the way, it was mishandled, and a person died as a result. David decided to leave it at Obed-Edom's house and retrieve it later. During the three months the ark was at his house, the Lord prospered Obed-Edom so much that David heard about it and wanted the ark brought back properly to Jerusalem and the temple where it was supposed to be.

I had always loved this story because of how God blessed Obed-Edom's whole household since he honored God by taking proper care of the ark of the covenant, which ushered in the presence of God. Obed-Edom is an example to me that God is fully aware of those whose hearts are completely His. His covenant with me because of the blood of Jesus is important to Him and He delights to bless those who honor Him. I see a correlation with this story and what Paul says in I Corinthians 16:9 that because of Jesus, our bodies are the temples of the Holy Spirit of God. We are the ark; we are the temple, and God's blessing is on us as we listen to Him and walk in His ways.

As we took care of and served many, many international students throughout the years, as we worshiped God with them, as we prayed with and for them, the blessing of the Lord was on our household. His presence could be felt. His peace permeated our property and brought great blessing to us and to all who came to our home. We were protected, covered financially, physically in great health, and blessed in every other way as we opened our hearts and lives to these students Jesus loved. We increased in multiple ways during this time because of the blessing of the Lord. And it all started with that first worship school we attended at Bethel.

We kept going back down to Redding every summer for seven years to attend the worship school. Casey and Kelcy both went with me the next six years, and as a family, we began attending conferences a couple times a year. We were learning and growing so much in experiencing God in ways we never had before, getting to know Him and love Him more deeply than ever.

STEVE BACKLUND - TWO KEYS

Kelcy and I were sitting in the sanctuary at Bethel that first summer in 2009 waiting for the Friday night service to begin. We attended every service we possibly could. We were like dry sponges just soaking up everything God offered us. One of the church leaders came up to us and introduced himself, asking us where we were from. We said we were from Ellensburg, Washington. He immediately lit up and told us his brother was a professor at Central Washington University in our town. He was so friendly and happy. He then gave us a book he had recently written about the power of our words, and we chatted a bit about Ellensburg.

A few months later we were back home. My mom was in a care facility in town and my sister, dad, my kids, and I would go once a week to sing Gospel songs and hymns as an activity that was open to all the residents in the center. As we were singing "How Great Thou Art," a gentleman poked his head in the room, then went right back out.

Kelcy and I looked at each other and I asked, *"Isn't that a Bethel pastor? That guy we met?"* How random that he would be in Ellensburg!

I remembered his name and that his brother and mother lived in Ellensburg, so I took off down the hallway looking at the name tags on every door. The final door had a tag with his surname, and there he was sitting in the room near his mother's bed. He came out into the hallway and we chatted for ten to fifteen minutes. Then he began to speak over me, talking about the work we were doing with international students and that the ministry God had called us to was much bigger than we thought. He also said God had two life keys for me on a "chain" around my neck: Gratitude and the Power of Words.

He gave Psalm 100:4-5 for Gratitude which says *"Enter His gates with Thanksgiving and into His courts with praise. Be thankful to Him and bless His name. For the Lord is good, His mercy is everlasting and His truth endures to all generations"* (NKJV). Thanksgiving is the door that opens the coming goodness of God.

For the Power of Words, he spoke Proverbs 18:21, *"Life and death are in the power of the tongue, and those who love it will eat its fruit"* (NKJV). Declarations are key. Then he said he saw the gift of faith on me, *"You are a woman of faith! Well you already have this and operate in it, but you are being catapulted to the next level—like a huge leap, a shift."* He also said he wanted to help us, to send interns up from Redding to help with our worship nights. And he did. We had a number of his amazing intern teams come up over the years and minister at our worship nights. They always had just the right word for our students and were full of love and grace.

FATHER'S DAY GIVING

Our first Father's Day Sunday at Bethel rocked my world. Pastor Bill Johnson invited all the men to stand up as he prayed over them. This was pretty standard in all the churches I had been in, so it came as no surprise. But then, after he had the fathers sit down, he asked all the single moms who were raising their children alone to stand. I perked up and paid attention because I had never seen this. He encouraged them, then had them hold out their hands to receive. He told the congregation to now go and bless these single moms with money. It was AMAZING! This was something I knew my church would never do, just have people give cash to others, and instantly I wanted to be a part.

I had begun taking cash for giving down to Bethel every time we would go. When I sensed God had someone in mind to give it to, I would. When those single moms stood with their hands out, I jumped up, grabbed some of that offering money and put it in the hands of several of the moms. So did many other people. Tears were streaming down their faces as their hands overflowed with cash. The blessing to my heart of giving this way was stunning. Watching others do the same was overwhelmingly beautiful. I knew I had found my tribe. This was a giving church. These were a people who wanted to be like their Heavenly Father who gave His most precious thing, who gave His Son and gave His heart. I was on track to becoming more like Him!

LOVE AFTER MARRIAGE

The first summer at Bethel, I watched all the church weekly announcements eagerly hoping there would be events we could come to as a family. I so wanted Clint and Casey to experience what Kelcy and I had. Sure enough, the fall of 2009, there was an Open Heavens conference that seemed perfect for our family. One of my first Heavenly Agreements was believing that we would be able to attend spirit-filled conferences—that we would have enough money to travel to different conferences we were interested in and money for hotel stays, food, and other extras. And here we were beginning to live in the reality I had been believing would happen.

From that first conference, many more followed. One of the most significant was Love After Marriage. We attended this week-long event in early October, 2010. It was for married couples and came with a significant registration fee, plus there would be the hotel and food costs added to that. We saved up and were able to meet the expenses. The kids came with us, so we prepped for a week of homeschool studies that the kids (who were in their teens) would be able to do on their own in the hotel. We also had friends in Redding who were able to check in with them from time to time.

The week beautifully changed our lives, bringing in the supernatural presence of God to our relationship. On Thursday, the hosts prayed over the men to dream dreams from the book of Joel 2:28 which says, *"And it will come about after this that I will pour out My Spirit on all mankind; and your sons and daughters will prophesy, your old men will dream dreams, your young men will see visions"* (NASB).

That night, Clint had a small vision of a ladle filled with beautiful red wine being offered. We took the vision to our small group at the conference and various members had different interpretations of what it might mean. Overall, the consensus was that God was inviting Clint and us into a deeper relationship with each other and Him. Just as Jesus turned water into wine at the wedding in Cana, we felt He was showing He was interested in our marriage, our family, and our life.

WHY ARE YOU SO HIDDEN?

The leaders of Love After Marriage, Barry and Lori, prayed over each of us at the last session. They prayed leadership and a spirit of Gideon over Clint, asked Clint if he was a farmer and asked me if I liked to cultivate things (I love gardening), asked if we had kids and said the whole family is covered by this thing–the Love of God. Then Lori turned to me and said in surprise, "*You've been invisible! No more! That's been the devil's work.*" And she spoke over me, breaking whatever the holding back was, then asked, "*Why are you so hidden?*" I kind of shrugged, but this is a question I had been asking God time and again throughout the years and hadn't received an answer. Lori didn't have an answer for me, either. Barry then encouraged me to get close to people when I went back home so I could share with them all I had learned at Love After Marriage.

We returned home wondering what would be next with God.

THE QUESTION

I was true to the promise I had made to myself and began questioning again why we seemed to still be hidden. Why couldn't others see what was in us, what we were capable of? I felt a sense of God's hand extending down out of Heaven and cupping it around us, shielding us for His purposes, protecting us until the right time for release. I sensed that when we were released, we would spin out. I saw all of us, our whole family, like whirling dervish super heroes–twirling, spinning super-fast, slashing at the enemy, chains being broken, people being set free, Satan's bondages destroyed. I didn't know when it would happen, but I knew it would as I waited on the Lord and connected my heart to His.

THE THREE HORSES DREAM

As we often invited international students to our home to enjoy farm life, we needed another horse to give horse rides. Most of the students had never ridden a horse in their lives, and it was a highlight for them when visiting a farm. I had been asking around for another horse for several months, and upon our return home from the marriage event, I received a call from the lady who ran the rescue horse organization in town. She had found what she deemed to be the perfect horse for us, a sorrel (reddish/brown) gelding, about twelve years old. The gal who owned him needed to move him on as quickly as possible.

I was busy getting settled after a week away and didn't call the gal with the horse until Wednesday of our return week. When I did call, I set up a meeting to see the horse for Thursday morning. Meanwhile, Wednesday was the day of the week the kids and I went to the Christian school to help my sister with the music for the weekly chapel. As I was walking out of the school that Wednesday morning,

I saw a sign posted on the school bulletin board asking for anyone who would want to work with the seventh and eighth grade students who had been in band. As the school couldn't find a band teacher, they were considering starting a worship team instead. Although the sign caught my attention, I had no interest in teaching seventh and eighth graders again. But when I got home, I just couldn't get the idea of teaching a worship team out of my mind, especially as we had completed two years of the summer worship school at Bethel at that point. I resisted the thought twice, but when it came back the third time, I knew it was God speaking to me. I reached out to the school principal and was asked to come in immediately to take over the class. I laughed and let her know I would talk to Clint and pray about it. She then asked if I would come in on Friday to meet with her and another potential teacher—the two of us could possibly split the class time and co-teach. I agreed to the Friday meeting.

When Clint got home Wednesday night, I told him about the Christian school worship team teacher job. We both were totally sure that this was NOT a place either of us wanted me to be. But because I sensed God on it, even though I was 99.9% sure I did not want the job, I felt we needed to ask God what He thought. I asked Clint if we could at least pray and ask God to give him a dream that would clarify things. He was open to that, so we prayed.

The next morning, Thursday, I was to meet the lady with the horse. Before Clint left for work, I asked him if he had had a dream. He said he had not one, but three dreams. In the first dream he was walking through our south field and passed three horses – one sorrel, one black, and one white. The white one stood out as it was a younger horse but looked old. The second dream took place down Main Street in Ellensburg. Clint was riding shotgun in a white dually pick-up truck and all the air in the tires went out. Clint told the driver not to worry about it, to drive the truck to Les Schwab and he would pay to get the tires aired up and on the road again. The third dream was one where Clint was fixing a fence in our back field which was adjacent to a neighbor's field.

The second I heard the dually pick-up dream I KNEW it was the Christian school and that God was saying I was to take this assignment. Many times in dreams vehicles represent ministries and being that the local Christian school had about one hundred students, this dually truck seemed about the right size to represent it. The air leaving the tires represented to me the breath of God and the Holy Spirit. God wanted to re-fill the school with His presence. This is something we had been learning about at the Bethel Worship schools. I knew that God was saying to Clint (and me) that we were to do this assignment at our own expense–bringing a shift into the school. Clint wasn't quite so convinced, so we tabled it and both went about our day.

The kids and I took off to visit the lady with the horse to see if this horse would fit with what we needed for international students. When we arrived, the lady met us and pointed out the horse, Cade, a sorrel quarter horse. She told me a little of his background, then pointed to another horse, Harley, (white) and asked if I would take that one, too, as he was young at six years old, not trained, but he had never been apart from the one she wanted us to have. She then pointed to a third horse (black) and asked if I would be willing to take that one, too. The third horse, Obie, was seventeen years old and one they had paid a lot of money for to use as a barrel racing horse for their daughter. But they were finished with horses. Her husband had said they were all too expensive and she needed to get rid of them. Well, I was pretty sure Clint would not be very happy if I brought home three horses. We already had two and that would give us five! That was a lot of horses, even for us.

I told her I would take the first horse and talk to Clint about the other two, then get back to her. As the kids and I were driving away, they asked, *"Hey, did Dad have a dream last night?"* as they knew about our dream challenge.

I said, *"Yes! He had three and in the first one he was walking through the south field and came across three horses, a sorrel, a black, and a white one that was young but looked old. Oh, my goodness! These are the three horses!"* I about shouted when I realized that the dream contained these very horses.

As it turned out, we did get all three, for free, and they were a wonderful addition to our farm and our little international student ministry. And I did end up taking the teaching job and helped launch the Christian school worship team (along with my kids) for two years—exactly what God wanted us to do.

THREE-PRONGED ATTACK

We began the adventure with our worship team start-up at the Christian school in October of 2010. As soon as I signed on to the job, the principal told me we had to have some kind of performance for the Christmas Special which was on December 3rd. There wasn't much time to pull anything together, especially with a partial week

off for Thanksgiving and another half-week for parent-teacher conferences. First, I found out what kind of band/worship team I had.
Our talent included one seventh grade full kit drummer, three seventh
grade snare drum players, two eighth grade untrained guitar player
wannabes, no keyboard players, one untrained eighth grade bass
player, and a couple seventh grade girls who wanted to try their hand
at singing, but were very shy. This "worship team" had previously been
the seventh and eighth grade band which the school had axed, so we
were starting from scratch.

I brought in three keyboards and we began to train the snare
drum players and the singers how to play three of the easiest chords.
We chose two simple worship songs, "Here I Am to Worship" by Tim
Hughes and "Amazing Love" by Chris Tomlin. I knew if I could get
the band to at least play the songs, I could have Casey (then ten years
old) play bass and Kelcy sing and play keys as well. We also had Jake,
the drummer, who was really good. If no one else but those three did
anything, we would be okay at the Christmas concert.

We knew how to worship as a family together and connect to the
heart and presence of God. The kids and I also had the experience
of leading worship and singing in the nursing home to fall back on.
We knew if we just closed our eyes and worshiped and didn't care
much about the sound or the outcome, God would show up. He had
done it before, He would do it again. We knew that His presence
changes everything.

Our little worship team practiced and practiced and practiced
those two songs. They actually sounded pretty good coming into the
concert on December 3rd. But two days before the concert, all hell

broke loose in our house. I knew immediately that this was demonic resistance because the atmosphere was shifting over the Christian school and the students were opening to God's heart, so there was resistance.

We personally had attacks with three different things. First off, our computer died—just quit working out of the blue. We very quickly came to realize how much we depended on that computer! I took it to get fixed but we were a week or so without it. The second thing that happened was credit card fraud. When our bill came in, we had about $700 in charges from a restaurant in Florida. We had never been to Florida and had not frequented a restaurant there either in person or online. I called the credit card company, began the process of removing the charges and setting up a new credit card for all our accounts. The final thing was that our heat went out. Completely. In the beginning of December. When it was very cold. We have a propane stove in our house, and it just quit. Clint worked it over but just couldn't get it started. The house was getting cold. I had several small electric heaters that I placed around the house but they didn't do much. It was Friday. The concert was Saturday, the next day.

On Fridays, our family had our personal worship night. I asked Clint if we could take a bit of time and just worship. He was reluctant to do that as he felt he needed to spend his time figuring out what was wrong with our heat. Eventually, he decided to join the kids and me in taking thirty minutes for worship. As we worshiped, Clint had a God-idea which he shared with us after. He thought of the two big furnaces he had in our shop that he used to dry sheet rock on his jobs. He figured he could rig one up in the house by connecting it to our electrical system, and even though it would be loud, it would produce enough heat to warm the whole house and give him time to figure out and fix the stove. So that's what he did so we had warmth that night.

THE CONCERT

At the concert on Saturday, we were all stunned at how God showed up for those two simple worship songs. Our little class was last to "perform," and the presence of God became tangible. Even though the girls who were supposed to sing on mic froze in the beginning, Kelcy carried it through and God came. I was sitting in the front middle in the concert hall to give the little team courage, to worship along with them, and to pray for them. The gentleman sitting next to me leaned over as they were singing and told me that this team was better than his own church's adult worship team. I was so proud of them!

After the concert, others came up to me and expressed amazement for what had been accomplished in less than a month and a half with this group of kids. But God! We were on the right track in filling up those tires with the breath of God, the wind of the Holy Spirit, in that white dually truck ministry of the Christian school.

PRAYER & ANOTHER ATTACK

The new year brought some more changes. We connected with one of the Christian school teachers, Patti, who had a heart for prayer. The kids and I began meeting after school with Patti and her daughter once a week to worship together and pray over the school. We loved those times of worship and seeking God together. We were seeing changes in the hearts of the students and a significant increase in the presence of God throughout the school, students and teachers alike.

But once again, the attack was on and we had three more negative events that we worked through. In January we had a cow die, a horse die (a rescue horse we had), and our rescue feral cat, Benny (who decided he liked us and quit being feral), was attacked by a couple other cats and needed veterinary care.

Again, it was very evident that what we were doing with prayer and worship at the Christian school was spiritually effective and the dark side didn't like it. Even though we took a hit financially with all this, we stayed true to the Word of God, knowing that we were in a place of obedience to God in our lives. We had planted good seed with our giving, and we had held fast to our confession, declaring His Word. We believed Job 36:11 that says if we obey and serve Him, we will spend our days in prosperity and our years in pleasures. Also Hebrews 10:23, *"Let us hold firmly to the confession of our hope without wavering, for He who promised is faithful"* (NAS).

THE INCREDIBLES

One night in January, we had a family movie night and decided to watch *The Incredibles*, a movie we had enjoyed before. As I was watching it, I thought, *"Yeah, that's me . . . that's US."* Each of us carried these amazing gifts, "super-God powers" and abilities that worked together so well when we ministered to and loved on our college international students as well as the ministry with the worship team at the Christian school. I listed in my journal on the 5th of January, 2011 what I saw that each of us carried:

Me: seer and feeler; gift of Faith; giver; strongly feel God's presence, then images come; I am the warrior not afraid of the battle and the fight.

Kelcy: dancing, singing–powerfully bringing His presence with dance and scarves and flags; Such a host of God's presence, His beauty and lovely fragrance; she transports people to heaven.

Casey: feels heat with the presence of God; musician; bass player who can break bondages and keeps the beat, keeps steady, connected to God's heartbeat.

Clint: carries depth and perception; He's a perceiver, bringer of security, stability, humor, steadiness, surety, purity, strength, and trustworthiness.

I was so moved by these thoughts that, after the family went to bed, I stayed up praying and connecting with the heart of God over my family. Then the thought came that we should go down to Bethel Church for Casey's birthday weekend at the end of January. I shared this the next morning and the kids got so excited, but Clint became concerned and reserved. I tried to talk it through with him, but that did no good. He really didn't want to go. He told me that the kids and I had a tighter connection with Bethel because we had been there for greater lengths of time. He told us the kids and I could go but he didn't see any sense in him going that far just for a weekend service. I suddenly had the thought that maybe there was something else going on over that weekend at Bethel, so I jumped on my computer and looked it up. Sure enough, there was a one-day Nutrition/Wellness seminar. I laughed out loud.

I showed it to Clint and suggested that Kelcy and I could go to the seminar and he and Casey could hang out with some friends in Redding. In fact, we could ask the friends and they would probably put us up for two nights so there would be no hotel costs for us. Clint was still not on board. I began to get discouraged and thought that perhaps I shouldn't go, but I felt God telling me that Kelcy and I should go to the Wellness seminar even if Clint wouldn't go. Then I had the idea to ask Clint if he would ask God for a sign to give clear indication because I felt we ALL needed to go because we are The Incredibles! We work best together. We function in our gifts and abilities best when we are connected. I asked Clint to pray and ask God for a sign on Saturday evening. He reluctantly did so.

SUNHEE

Sunday morning, I got up early and checked email while Clint was out feeding the cows. I got a little confused because there was an email with the subject line: "Redding and Bethel Church" from Sunhee, a Korean friend who was a previous international student at CWU. We had befriended Sunhee and her daughter while they were in Ellensburg for a year and had become close. Here is the email I received that Sunday morning in Sunhee's own words:

Hi Becky!

How have you been?

I am so happy to receive your card and Kelcy's 'The Swanstrum News 2010'. It was another pleasure for me to read your hand writing card. Kelcy's letter reminded me the beautiful life in Ellensburg last year.

Last week I read a book written by Eo Ryung Lee who was the first Ministry of Culture in Korea. The book is a kind of his testimony why he became a Christian when he was over 75 years old. It's a very impressive book. He was smart and intellect but he didn't know God and was proud of himself. However, he was changed because of his daughter. His lovely daughter got through hard times such as divorce, cancer, lost [sic] of see-sight and her son's ADHD and autism. After she became a Christian and felt God's unthirsty love. Then, she experienced God's miracle that her cancer and her son's disease were completely cured. Her long prayer for father and his love toward the daughter made him change his mind.

While I was reading the book, I was surprised to find the words 'Redding and Bethel church' where Kelcy, Casey and you went for learning worship dance last summer. In the book, his daughter had an private experience to meet Jesus at a Hotel room in Redding. She said that she just went there for spending summer vacation. At that time, she lived in CA and she didn't know that there was a famous place where miracles and wonders often happen. After I finished reading the book, I searched the information about the church and the paster [sic] Bill Johnson. It was interesting to know the powerful church. I want to visit there someday if I have a chance.

I love you and miss you! I hope you have always wonderful time.

With love,

Sunhee

I pretty much started crying and laughing at the same time. This is what I had been trying to tell Clint the night before, that going to Bethel wasn't just about attending a church service miles away. Bethel was a place where the people had contended for God's presence so much that there was an open heaven over the city and even over the entire region. It was a place where it was easy for anyone to connect with God, full of peace, so life-giving.

When Clint came in from feeding, I about knocked him over with my email news. Clint did see that this was the sign God was giving him. We went the next weekend. We were graced for the trip and it was good. The nutrition seminar was awesome. We connected with a couple families. But most importantly, Clint and I connected with each other. We were able to talk together in such a good and satisfying way. It was like the Love After Marriage conference all over again. Clint was at peace, open, and enjoying the adventure. I was so happy. It was an amazing trip, for sure. The blessing of God was abundant upon our family.

TREMENDOUS ACCESS TO THE THRONE ROOM

The kids and I kept going down to Bethel every summer, year after year, and by the fourth year we were helping regularly with the summer kids' ministry camp program. The week-long camp was about an hour out of Redding. Our first year was Casey's final year as a camper since he was twelve and would age out the next summer. Kelcy was a counselor assistant, and I helped with the decorating and general flow of the Encounter Room.

The Encounter Room was a place where kids would come with their cabin groups to encounter the presence of God. There were quiet, exploratory activities and time and space for the kids to meet with Jesus. It was a wonderful place. I loved searching the creative heart of God to know how to put the materials, furnishings, and crafts together to create this space. Laura, the children's pastor from Bethel, had the vision, and it was a huge joy to help her each summer.

As soon as the camp week was over, we would return to Redding and hang out a few days before heading back home to Washington. We enjoyed going to Bethel's Saturday morning Healing Rooms. There the sanctuary was turned into a giant Encounter Room with live worship soaking music, places to enjoy the presence of the Lord by lying down, sitting, enjoying personal communion, praying with others, watching the prophetic artists at work, and just listening to God.

Casey and I were sitting in the large encounter room one Saturday morning enjoying the worship when one of the leaders came up to us. We knew the gentleman from previous visits to the Healing Rooms and also from kids' camp. I remember he was wearing a pink shirt that day. He took Casey's hand high-five style and began speaking over him. He exclaimed,

"*Your hand is on fire, glory is all over you two! You are so anointed! Do you ever pray for the sick?*"

Casey answered, "*Sometimes.*"

He replied, "*Well, do it more because as you do people will get healed.*"

He then turned to me, high-fived my hand and said to Casey,

"*Whoa, your mother is AMAZING!*" To me he said,

"*You are a friend of God! You have tremendous access into the Throne Room!*"

After several times saying that, he went on his way. My immediate thought was, '*Of course I do!*' This is something I have known for a very long time. I am so confident that God hears me when I call, that I can go whenever I want to spend time with Him in the Throne Room, that I am received instantly by Him, and that I am always welcome to come into His presence. What this gentleman telling me this did for me was it strengthened my heart that I was noticed by God, and what was in me was so big it was noticed by others, too. I thought that maybe one day I would have a voice to share the wisdom of God in me to others. I thought maybe, just maybe, I would no longer feel like I was hidden. I was so grateful and honored that God had picked us out from all the people in that room to encourage us and to let us know He saw our hearts, He saw our intercession, our generosity, and He was supporting us all the way.

RAINBOWS

As we continued to pour out our hearts, home, finances, and lives to the many international and American students we met, there began to be many sightings of rainbows. Sometimes we would have a group of students coming for a cooking class and we would look out the window to see a beautiful rainbow. Instantly, every camera came out and many pictures were taken. We might be giving horse rides and sure enough, there would be a rainbow and those cameras were at it again!

I realized this was God's covenant promise to me and to us as a family. It was in my special song that I loved as a two-year-old, '*The Lord sends the rainbow to follow the rain'* and it is the sign of His covenant in Genesis 9:12-16. *"This is the sign of the covenant which I am making between Me and you and every living creature that is with you, for all successive generations; I set My bow in the cloud, and it shall be for a sign of a covenant between Me and the earth. It shall come about, when I bring a cloud over the earth, that the bow will be seen in the cloud, and I will remember My covenant, which is between Me and you and every living creature of all flesh . . . When the bow is in the cloud, then I will look upon it, to remember the everlasting covenant between God and every living creature of all flesh that is on the earth"* (NASB).

It became clear that rainbows were God's special sign to us of His pleasure and covenant with us–that He was noticing as we poured out His love to these students.

One Sunday morning, I got a text from my friend Becky who lived in Redding. It said this:

"Hey beck! Thinking about you. Saw you raising your hands to heaven and a rainbow formed between them. It grew wider as you spread your arms. You joined your rainbow with an Asian woman who also had a rainbow in her arms and it spread like a blanket over a multitude of people."

Whoa! I was blown away. I thought perhaps the Asian woman was even my Korean friend, Sunhee, or it could have been symbolic of all the beautiful Asian students we had befriended and ministered to. It was another confirmation by God, 'El Roi', *the God who sees* (Genesis 16:13) that we were seen, noticed, and known by the only One who mattered, and His blessing was on us and our household. We always had enough even as we were giving so much away.

THE TRAIN DREAM

About this time, Clint had another dream. In this one, he was running along the top of a long freight train, jumping from car to car. The feeling was one of adventure, kind of like an *Indiana Jones* vibe. What came out of this for us was that God was using us as a 'train ministry' where we had ministry into many, many different areas: international students with worship nights, home stays, cooking classes, helping with getting apartment supplies and The Storehouse; our involvement in church worship teams and children's ministry; teaching worship at the Christian school, and much more. We were not supposed to be a 'pulpit ministry' but just living out our lives and being ministers of His Kingdom in how we lived wherever we were.

A few days after Clint's train dream, the kids and I were at the dining room table doing school work, and Casey's Language Arts lesson was on conjunctions. I remembered these cute videos I had seen when I was in school to help remember different language, math, history and other facts, and I looked them up online because I knew there was one about conjunctions. The videos were through *Schoolhouse Rock* and the name of the one I was looking for was "Conjunction Junction." I quickly found it and began playing it. The scene was a train yard with trains coming and going, train cars hooking up with one another, then moving out of the train yard while the words were being sung about conjunctions. Each train car connection would have a conjunction word, such as 'and', 'but', and 'or'. As I watched the trains moving in and out of the yard, I suddenly heard and felt God confirming that THIS was our ministry. Each car represented a different part of the ministry God had called us to, and as we completed each assignment, the cars just kept being added on and on and on. It was an awesome picture and very satisfying to know that, once again, God saw us and was aware of our hearts toward Him and the people He had called us to serve. We knew He would never leave us or forsake us and we would always have more than enough to fulfill the call of God on our lives.

APPLE CARE

The year was 2014 and there had been a complete upheaval of the medical system for the whole country. Obamacare, otherwise known as The Affordable Care Act, had begun in 2010, but it wasn't until 2014 that it was enforced, and all Americans were required to have insurance coverage or face fines. Although we had been carrying medical and hospital insurance for our family, when the Act kicked in, that insurance became too expensive and we couldn't afford it any longer. I began looking into alternatives. We settled on a lower grade insurance for the duration while we continued to 'shop' for other options.

Meanwhile, we got a letter in the mail from our state medical insurance program for both our kids. A program known as Apple Care was free to us until the kids turned nineteen. Kelcy was eighteen, so she had one year before she aged out of the program. But Casey had four years to enjoy the benefits. Since we rarely had any medical issues, I actually was offended that our kids had been put on this program. I thought it was for much lower income families and that we were put on by mistake or some glitch in the system. Looking back, with our monthly salary, we definitely did qualify.

As it turned out, it was a HUGE blessing because when Casey was sixteen, he went to work with Clint on the job site one day, tried to pull a piece of rebar out of the ground and took a tumble, landing on his arm. He complained of it hurting him a bit, but we wrapped it and figured it was bruised, but nothing more. He even went to the county fair that week several times with his friends and seemed to be fine.

But after the fair was over, he began complaining that the arm didn't seem to be getting any better, so we had it x-rayed and, sure enough, he had broken it. He had broken it on the growth plate of his wrist, so it was a pretty significant break. We ended up at an orthopedic surgeon in Yakima forty minutes away. They scheduled him for surgery. He had a pin put in and spent a night in the hospital, which he loved because of the free food and TV time! The break healed cleanly but took the required number of weeks and several changes of casts before he got a clean bill of health.

The remarkable thing was that we paid nothing—not for the x-rays, not for the doctor's visits, not for the surgery, and nothing for the hospital stay. If the Affordable Care Act had not been passed when it was, we would have had significant bills to pay. But we only paid one $30 premium that year. Of course, our tax dollars helped pay for that program, but we benefited from it in a huge way. God definitely worked all things together for our good in that case! (Romans 8:28)

GIVING DESIRE GROWS

During this time our desire to see an increase in our giving continued to grow. We had moved past $10 givers and up to $100 givers consistently, with $1,000 giving thrown in here and there. We were able to give more each time we gave because of the blessing of the Lord.

Then the day came when we were able to move up to the $10,000 level. It happened in Kelcy's second year at BSSM. She was on one of the four second year worship teams. It was an awesome team, fully connected and loving each other. Casey and I would go down to visit Kelcy and were always invited to the team breakfasts and get-togethers. It was an awesome time of fellowship, sharing and loving on these amazing students from all over the world.

That spring, the planned mission trip for everyone in the second year school (around 900 students) was a special event hosted by Lou Engle and The Call in Los Angeles. The group was split into their revival groups with their pastors and would be ministering for a couple days all around the city, then the event would culminate at the Rose Bowl for a mighty intercession cry over the nation. Each student had to fund their trip, and God put it on our hearts to pay for Kelcy's entire second year worship team to go. This cost was close to $12,000 for the hotel, food, and travel necessities. We had the money saved and gave it all. It was so exciting to see we had managed to move up another level. Of course, all our giving from that point on was not at that level, but once we "broke the barrier," it was easier to believe God for the next time He asked us to give.

There have been several other times recently we have been able to give at the $4,000, $5,000 and $10,000 level, and it is always an amazing thing to watch the blessing of the Lord that comes with that kind of obedience and extravagant (for us) giving. We are still moving toward the $100,000 level of giving. We haven't been there yet, but we know it will happen!

I have often wondered at people who talk about their life verse. Looking for a *life* verse has never really resonated with me. But through all of this giving journey, it has become clear that I *do* have a life verse in Proverbs 10:22 which says: "*The blessing of the Lord makes one rich, and He adds no sorrow with it*" (NKJV).

Chapter 6

TAKING STOCK

I was 2017. Kelcy was down in Redding enjoying a gap year after attending three years of BSSM. Clint and I decided to go down for a Thanksgiving visit as Kelcy was working and had limited time for travel. Casey was in his first year at Central Washington University with tests and projects due immediately after Thanksgiving break, so it wasn't a good time for him to take a trip. We all decided he could stay home, feed the cows, take care of the farm, and get his studying and projects done while Clint and I drove down to Redding.

In preparing for the trip, we made lists for Casey of chores and responsibilities to do while he was home. While doing this, it came to our attention that if something happened to us while we were on the road (‘*Expect the best, but prepare for the worst!*’), Casey and Kelcy would need help. They would need to know all the people to contact for each part of our lives. And there were a lot of parts.

Our lists got longer and longer. We had the construction business, Swanstrum Construction Inc., which would need to be managed and closed, especially since Clint was in the middle of a house building project. We had the farm with thirty-five to forty cows and calves that would need to be taken care of. We had horses that would need to be cared for. We had our will and all the legal aspects of our lives. Casey needed to know who to contact for help with each of these parts of our lives, as well as who the Executrix was of our will and what our wishes were. He needed to know where our safe was, what was in it, and the lock combination. There was the property and house we lived in, the Lone Pine twenty-seven acre property that was being managed by a local farmer, and two condos in Redding, one lived in by Kelcy, one being rented. The kids would need to know what to do with those. They would need to know about property taxes, insurances, bank accounts, retirement accounts, and investment accounts. There were so many aspects of our lives that up to this point we had managed, but the kids had been busy with their lives, so we had never walked them through step-by-step what to do if we were gone tomorrow.

I began making up two lists—one to leave with Casey and one to take to Kelcy. As I was doing this, I was putting together the monetary value of each of these things we owned and managed and was astounded to see that we had crossed the million-dollar mark.

At this point, we knew our net worth was demanding we find help managing it all. We needed to know if we had the proper amount of insurance coverage and if our Will was adequate to cover and represent what we wanted.

When we safely arrived back home after that trip, a Seattle friend contacted me. We had met fifteen years before when we were attending the Seattle church, and our families had grown close. From time to time, we would each drive an hour to meet halfway for a visit. This time, Mariana and Paul invited us to their home for an overnight stay to touch base and visit. We needed to deliver some beef to the West side anyway, so we decided to spend a night with them. Through the years, we had watched these friends struggle financially trying to find what really fit their passions. We had supported them with gifts, cash cards, winter coats for their kids when they couldn't afford them, and more. Paul had even lived with us in Ellensburg for a semester while he finished up his degree at CWU. During that time, Clint had hired him to help with a house build he was working on.

Although I had touched base with Mariana over the years, it had been some time since we had seen Paul. In the intervening years, they had gone to Michigan where Paul had obtained his law degree specializing in estate planning. Once finished, they had moved back to the Seattle area. We had known estate planning was Paul's specialty, but never felt a need to reach out to him with our estate because we already had a will and didn't think we had enough assets to go any further. We had made the will when the kids were very young and hadn't looked at it since, but we felt secure because we had one.

We got to Paul and Mariana's place and, during our visit, broached the subject of my dad's will. At this point, my dad couldn't mentally understand much and I was his Durable Power of Attorney. I wanted to make sure everything was in order. Paul told me to send him a copy and he would look it over. From that conversation, we began talking about our own assets. It was very clear to both Clint and me that we needed to take the next step and work with Paul and his law firm, *Planning With Purpose*, to make sure we were set up the way we wanted to be and our assets were secure. We made an appointment to meet.

Later on, when Paul looked at our will, we were so glad God had prompted us to take this step because the way it was written was that if either Clint or I had passed away, all the assets, except for household furnishings, would have gone to the kids. No monetary assets would pass on to the living spouse. What a mess! Needless to say, we began the process of re-doing our will correctly by putting all our assets into a Swanstrum Family Trust which was created on February 20, 2018.

Paul's practice takes an interactive approach with clients. Each year we meet and go over the trust and our desires. It is easy to make changes if we need to. We have come to realize how valuable it is to keep up-to-date with estate planning and how it is key to good stewardship. Once again, we saw how God orchestrated us to being in the right place at the right time for His purposes and blessing on our lives. We never would have thought of all this in such detail on our own. It is so good to be led by the Holy Spirit in EVERY area of life.

We have given attention to managing our resources well these past few years, as we continue to see and understand how important stewardship is to God. While there are many verses in the Bible about how to do life well, there are over 2,300 pertaining to money. Compare this to around 500 on faith and prayer, over 100 healing scriptures, over 296 verses dealing with angels, 200+ about the poor, and the list goes on. A full 40% of Jesus' parables deal with stewardship and money. How we handle money is very important to God! Stewarding what He has given us and giving well has become very important to us as well.

EVERY DAY MILLIONAIRES

In the summer of 2018, Clint and I were listening to a Dave Ramsey podcast where he invited people who had crossed the million-dollar mark to text his team and let them know. They wanted to publish the stories of "Every Day Millionaires" in hopes of encouraging others to do the same. Clint and I are somewhat private introverts, but for some reason, we thought, '*Why not?*' I texted the number, gave the information they asked for, and then forgot about it.

In December, the Ramsey team reached out to us wanting to know our story for the purpose of putting us on their social media. It was exciting to see how far we had come, and we gave all glory to

God. We were and are so grateful for His leading and guidance in our lives, for granting us many opportunities to give generously, and showing Himself faithful to us over the years. He had done above and beyond anything we could have asked or thought. We shared our story.

Here is what the team posted on Instagram and Facebook on March 4, 2019:

Clint and Becky are a great example of what it looks like to take personal responsibility for your future. Here is their story:

"When we married 25 years ago, I was 38 and Clint was 32. I had been a school teacher barely scraping by, and Clint was working for a contractor with hourly wages. We bought the farm Clint was raised on directly from his mom with the hope of paying it off in 7 years. We had no other debt. Our household income at that time was around $40,000 per year.

Five years and two kids later, we realized we needed to do something for retirement since we had nobody else doing it for us. By this time Clint had gotten his contractor's license and I was a stay-at-home mom. We began learning everything we could on building wealth. We changed some things - whole life insurance to term life, found an amazing financial planner, set up retirement accounts, 529s and UTMAs for our kids, and selling everything we could to make money.

Then, Clint received a $200,000 inheritance from a family member that we distributed into those accounts. Because of compound interest and saving consistently, we hit millionaire status by 2012 - seven years from when we started to do something.

Then, we heard of Dave Ramsey and attended Financial Peace University at our church. We loved it and went at our plan with gazelle intensity - even though we were already millionaires! We kept investing, buying land and 2 condos with cash, selling when the timing was right, living below our means, ALWAYS driving used cars, consistently tithing and giving extravagantly.

We pretty much live the same as we always have - same house that Clint was born and raised in, enjoying some extras like a trip to Hawaii last year, but no one would even guess our wealth. Currently at the end of 2018 our household income (which is the highest we've had) is around $80,000 and our net worth is 1.7 million.

Advice to others would be to not stress out even if you are starting later in life . . . Just START, be consistent, invest the maximum, be generous and stay out of debt!"

After this was posted, there were lots of people who congratulated us and told us that our story inspired them. But there were a few naysayers who said that of course we could finish well because of the inheritance of $200,000 from Clint's Uncle George. They said they could have done the same thing if money like that came their way.

That kind of fired me off, and I would like to set the record straight here. We managed that money well. We did not go out and buy new cars or clothes, houses, or upgrades in extravagant things. We already had accounts set up that we immediately deposited it into. We had a plan and we followed it.

But the most significant thing we have done throughout our married life is to give and give extravagantly. As of this date, we can document that we have given away well over $400,000 to individuals, families, and organizations. We gave as God directed us to give, even when it was a sacrifice (which it often was), even when we could have used the very thing we gave away. We have had people tell us to stop giving because it makes them look bad, that the money we give to others most people would use for themselves. Some say that we are very unusual. Others tell us we are an inspiration. We don't give to receive any accolades. We give in connection to His Voice. That is our confidence and our joy.

RESULTS OF GENEROSITY

Perhaps my greatest desire as we poured ourselves into others' lives was to bring encouragement and lasting change. I wanted to be the stair step for others to be able to go to the next level, to become all they could possibly be in God, to get solidly on the road to their destinies. I wanted to see those younger than me and Clint reach forward and attain what we took many years to learn and attain. I wanted to see them at thirty and forty years old doing what it took us until our fifties and sixties to see and do with finances and giving. The following letter is from one of our wonderful college students, Jack, whose life we had an impact on:

January 13, 2018

Hi Becky! I hope you're all doing well this winter! I just wanted to send you the biggest thank you letter that I can. Everything that you sacrificed and gave to me over the years has been on my mind lately and I just really wanted to send a message thanking you for all that you and your family has given to me. I am who I am today in large part to the powerful influence you and your family has had on me. I continue to be exceedingly grateful for all that you did for me while I was living in Ellensburg. All of it flowed from your lavish generosity for which I will never forget and truly cannot begin to express how grateful I am. The last couple of weeks as I've been driving to and from work, I keep thinking about truly how much you gave me and what a complete and utter gift from God you and your family have been in my life. God used you to shape my future in ways I won't know until I ask Jesus in Heaven. Thank you for your patience with me, your grace, your lavish generosity, and your love. I cherish these things and take none of them for granted. You have a powerful impact on so many people's lives, I am so very thankful that I got to be one of those people. Your wisdom you gave me over those years will stick with me for years to come. I really want you to know that every conversation, every time you took time out of your day to talk to me, has had a powerful impact on my relationship with Jesus. Your imparted wisdom truly has given me a better life, and will continue to shape how I pursue God. Thank you, Becky, for being a spiritual mother to me. Thank you for financially supporting me through your dad's condo and (my friend's) my trip to Kenya and in ways I probably can't even remember. These are generosities I will never forget. I am exceedingly grateful to you, your family, and God for how much you have given me. You have been the prime example in my life of how a family should pursue Jesus. Thank you—a thousand times thank you!

~Jack

As I re-read his email, I was struck at how much of the generous amounts of time, money, counsel, free housing, and more I had forgotten that we had given. For instance, I had forgotten about Jack's Kenya trip. He and Melvin had gone on a short mission trip to Kenya. We prayed over them at one of our Friday night Worship Nights, blessed them financially, and sent them on their way. A couple weeks into their trip we got a call from Jack that they were stuck in Kenya without resources to return home. We were in Redding visiting Bethel at the time, and I remember clearly that we needed to go to Wal-Mart to get a money order to wire $1,000 to Jack and Melvin so they could get out of the country. It all worked well and they arrived safely home. Another blessing given.

Jesus said in Matthew 6:3, "*But when you give to someone in need, do not let your left hand know what your right hand is doing*" (NLT). When a giving memory pops up, I laugh because this is exactly what we have been doing. We tend to forget the giving once it is done. We have given away so much in terms of finances to help others in their times of need that it takes a concentrated effort to remember the details of what we have given. Many times, it takes someone to remind us. So many lives have been impacted because we have lived with an open hand. We have chosen to represent God's heart to those around us here on the earth.

Another example follows. I had moved my father to an assisted living home and had his condo available for a year while waiting to see if we would be able to move dad back into his own living space. I felt the hand of God on offering dad's condo free-of-charge to Jack. It encouraged my heart to see that we truly were having positive and eternal impact on others as we walked hand-in-hand with the desires and purposes of Father God.

Here is another message from Jack in November, 2020:

Something I've been wanting to tell you about your generosity, that I've really only fully realized recently, is the exceeding spiritual worth it has been in my life. Regularly when I've been in a tough place where I'm heavily leaning into and needing God's provision, I think about staying in your Dad's condo. That continues to be a bulwark of God's steadfast love toward me — a complete physical representation of His provision that exceeds all I could ask or imagine. All that you and Clint have given me over the years bolsters my faith, but that condo is one of God's beautiful Crown Jewels of Providence in my life that is of exceeding spiritual significance. With great frequency God points to that wonderful house as a reminder of His constancy, faithfulness, and love toward me. Your giving over the years is as the very hands of God meeting my needs. It never ceases to point me toward Christ and deepen my trust in His perfect provision. These gifts didn't simply end with the provision met, but never ever cease to produce fruit in my life and draw me closer to Jesus. What you have given has an eternal place in my story. Only God can take something physical and turn it into something of eternal worth — I'm utterly amazed at the spiritual impact of giving. Thank you for your faithfulness Becky!

During the years that Jack was involved with our family, we also had a number of other college students who called our house their second home. These American students would come and join the international students for our weekly worship nights where we fed them, listened to them, prayed with them, and supported them in whatever ways we could.

One of those ways was to take students down to Bethel in Redding for Single Life workshops. Before we owned our own place in Redding, we would rent rooms from friends, or book hotel rooms and bring a load of students down for a week or weekend to experience the presence of God as we had in that wonderful place. We would also pay the fees for our students to attend these life-giving workshops. One of the workshops was a Believability School with Steve Backlund and Paul Manwaring. We had quite a group of students who wanted to go, so Clint drove one car with a full load and I drove another. We got two hotel rooms—one for the boys and one for the girls—in the hopes of seeing lives transformed.

About that time, we purchased the first condo in Redding. A sweet gal I was mentoring in Ellensburg was experiencing a very difficult time in her life. Her brother has passed away recently and the grief of it was just too much for her, so she dropped out of college at CWU. She lived in our shop apartment for a couple quarters and even worked for Clint in the beginning stages of building a house for one of his clients. She learned a lot and was able to process much of her pain with the manual labor that provided, but she needed spiritual nourishing as well.

It was the perfect fit for her to move into our brand-new condo in Redding. She was able to soak in God's love through attending Bethel Church while continuing to process her journey. We bought the place in April, and she moved in in May. When Kelcy moved down to Redding for her first year at BSSM in September, she had a built-in roommate with this sweet gal. They lived together for a year or so rent-free, which was a great blessing to both. We were able to pay for her to attend the Bethel School of Supernatural Ministry as well.

We were so glad to have been able to bring so many twenty-some-things down to Bethel and into this place of incredible healing and peace. We continue to pray for these young people as they now near their thirties and are getting married and settling down with families of their own. We believe that their destinies in God are mighty and

His plans for them will continue to unfold in miraculous ways–spiritually, mentally, socially, physically, and financially. They were all brought in as part of our family, and once a part of our family, always a part of our family!

TITHING FORWARD

In January of 2019, I drove down to Redding for Casey's birthday. He was playing bass on his 1st year worship team and I was able to be a guest visitor in his BSSM class. He introduced me to his teammates, one of whom was Naomi, a co-leader, who had been placed on his team for a few weeks. When he introduced her, he said, "*This is Naomi, she's 18.*"

I had no idea what he meant by that, but that's pretty much how Casey talks, so I let it slide. THEN worship started and when Naomi began to sing, all heaven opened up over me. I was blown away at how I felt the presence of God and was brought to tears. After the set, I told Casey how amazing I thought she was and he said, "*I know, that's why I told you she's 18.*"

That was a Thursday.

Casey's team also led on Monday, which in all our eleven years of going down to Bethel and visiting BSSM classes, has never happened where one team would play back-to-back two days in a row. But God! This time when Naomi started to sing, I heard God so clearly say, "*I want you to buy her some in-ears*" (in-ear monitors for worship teams so they can hear exactly what instruments and vocals they need to hear during the set).

I thought, '*Sure, that's about $100. I can order them on Amazon.*' But then I heard Him say, "*I want you to buy her CUSTOM in-ear monitors.*"

Well, that upped the ante because custom in-ear monitors can run anywhere from $1200 to $2000 plus! But I am ever obedient and am also very confident in hearing His Voice, so I said Yes. After worship, there was extended ministry time. I watched Naomi and really saw her heart. She was on her knees quietly crying out to the Lord like Hannah in the Old Testament when she was praying to have a child. God heard Hannah and gave her Samuel, who she then entrusted back to the Lord.

After the class, I went to Naomi and began asking her questions about her living situation, her family, her finances, and more. Even I was surprised at how forthright I was being with this sweet girl. But she answered every question and was continually tearing up with each one. Each answer she gave, God was telling me, "*I want you to pay that. And pay that, and pay for that.*"

I was adding it all up in my head and thinking, this is like $4,000! We got to the last question and I asked her about her in-ear monitors, wondering if she had her own. At this point, she began to downright cry and said she had been borrowing a friend's and they broke that very day. I laughed inside thinking how amazing God is. Then I told her we would pay for the rest of her school, her mission trip, her room and board through the end of the school year, and custom in-ears for her. It was amazing to see and feel the hand of God in all this. I told Clint later when I touched base with him that it felt like we were 'tithing forward', that God was having us give the 10% in advance of something.

Later we learned from Naomi's parents that Naomi had spent the last of her money for her February room and board. They had told her there was no more and she would have to come home at the end of February. The night before, her mom felt God telling her that it would be all right and not to worry.

After I talked with Naomi, she called her parents, and it was 2 a.m. in the U.K. She was screaming, crying, and shouting about what God had done. The next week, Naomi was assigned back to her regular worship team. She had only been on Casey's team for one month–the month I "happened" to be visiting.

Two months later, we sold the first condo we had bought in Redding, the one Kelcy had lived in when she attended first year BSSM. The amount we received was $40,000 over what we would have expected in that market. We had unknowingly given 10% of what our actual increase turned out to be! I am still in awe and amazed at how God orchestrated this financial increase miracle.

That day in January, 2019, as Casey and I were walking away from talking with Naomi about paying for the rest of her school expenses, Casey said, *"I'm so glad that happened, so people can see who WE are."*

I was so honored and grateful to hear this. That one statement was worth it all–priceless. It was completely God's blessing and kiss to me saying Clint and I had done well in our giving, that our example had been internalized by our son, and he saw extravagant giving as part of who he was, not just something his parents did. Passing on our heart and this mindset was more important than anything else we could have possibly done for our kids. It meant the world to me.

DEARDORFF HOUSE

Clint came home from work and said he had seen Sandi earlier that day. He had built a house for Sandi and her husband, Duane, a number of years before and kept in touch as they saw Clint as a surrogate son. They just loved him. This particular day, Sandi had told Clint that as she was cutting Martha Deardorff's hair, Martha had told her they would be selling their house and moving to the West side (Seattle area) to be closer to their son. They were getting older, approaching their mid-nineties, Martha's husband Stan had lung cancer, and it was time for them to be closer to family. They had lived in Ellensburg for thirty-five or so years, right next door to Clint's aunt and uncle's house, which then became his mom's house when Clint and I got married. The Swanstrums had known the Deardorffs for many years.

When Clint mentioned the Deardorffs would be selling their house and moving, Casey casually said, "*You guys should buy that house.*"

I immediately thought, "*Why?*" We had a house. We were out of debt completely and I didn't see any point in owning another house. There seemed to be no good reason to take it on. But over the next few days it became clear that God was on this in some way. First of all, Stan and Martha were struggling with poor health, and being as they had lived in the house for thirty-five years, there was a lot to be done including packing, cleaning, and painting, to get it sellable. That said, Stan had kept the house and property in excellent shape through the years, even with his illness and dementia setting in. They had never had pets and were not smokers. Martha had taken good care of the inside of the house, and even though it was a bit dated, it could be a good, solid purchase.

We made a call to them to see if selling the house to us would be something they might consider. Before we met with them, we sat down and counted the cost, keeping in mind Luke 14:28-30 which says, "*For which of you, desiring to build a tower, does not first sit down and count the cost, whether he has enough to complete it? Otherwise, when he has laid a foundation and is not able to finish, all who see it begin to mock him, saying, 'This man began to build and was not able to finish.'*"

Our counting the cost included the financial cap of what we could afford, if we were to enter into negotiating. We realized that we would need to borrow money to take out a mortgage, which neither of us found enticing. But by now, it was clear to both of us that this really was an assignment from God. Things moved along very quickly from that point.

We met with Stan and Martha. Stan presented his price and it was exactly what Clint and I had agreed was our top price point. We felt very strongly that Stan and Martha should not have to do anything to the house (new paint, carpet cleaning, updates, etc.), and that they could stay in it and rent it back from us however long they needed until they found their next place to live. All was agreed.

We put together a sales agreement, opened up escrow with a local title company, found a lender for the loan we would need to take, and began the process. Everything was smooth sailing, even to the point that we had a young couple wanting to rent the place as soon as the Deardorffs moved out. That was very nice. I liked having the security of knowing we would be financially covered from the get-go.

Having debt hanging over our heads again was not so nice. Most certainly we know the truth of the verse in Proverbs 22:7 that says, *"The rich rules over the poor, and the borrower is slave to the lender."* We also know the feeling of being that kind of slave. Because we had lived debt-free since 2012 when everything including our mortgage was paid off, it was not comfortable being in debt again, even for a house that would appreciate in value. But we trusted God and that we heard His voice.

After Stan and Martha moved out and the young couple moved in, things were going smoothly for a while. We had set a rent amount that we figured would cover us with the monthly mortgage, taxes, and insurance. It was a fair amount, but the couple renting the place preferred a lower rent. Since we couldn't go any lower, we suggested to them that they might want to take part of the house and make it into an Airbnb. The gal had run an Airbnb before for someone else, so she knew the ropes. We even came in and built a wall between the main living space and the Airbnb space so their living space and the rental space would be completely separate and secure. The house was built perfectly for this type of set-up.

On about the one-year mark, I began hearing some rumblings that insurance companies didn't particularly like Airbnb rentals and were hesitant to insure houses used as Airbnbs. In fact, some companies weren't just hesitant, they refused to insure them at all. A caution flag went up for me, and I began to do more research. I found that our insurance company for all our properties, cars, and business would not insure an Airbnb. The house had been insured by that company when it was a regular rental for one family, but since we had changed it to serving a dual purpose, our company would no longer insure it. We began looking for another company. Our renters began looking for another company. Neither of us could find anything that would insure a rental that was being used as an Airbnb by the renter. At this point, the couple decided to move and turn the house back over to us.

I was stressing for three months on what to do with the house. Should we rent it to a single family? Should we sell it? Should we continue using it as an Airbnb with me running it? I lost much sleep as I stressed over each scenario. I was not trusting God and my ability to hear His voice. But Clint was more practical and stable. He kept reassuring me that I could do it. He kept asking me what I wanted to do. Finally, we made the decision to turn the whole house into two Airbnb units and see what would happen.

We took over the house as an Airbnb the end of September, 2019. While we were running the original unit as an Airbnb, we were working on fixing up the second larger unit. We replaced the thirty-five-year-old carpets in the bedrooms and hallway. We replaced the main carpeted bathroom floor with tile and used the same tile to replace the worn-out carpet under the dining room table. We painted the whole place inside, then furnished it.

THE FURNISHINGS

Furnishing the Airbnb house contains more stories of the goodness of God and His leading in our lives. It started back a few years.

One day in 2009, I received a phone call from a friend, Laura, who had done children's ministry at the Foursquare Church with us years before. She told me she was working as a receptionist for a doctor and a gal had come in for an appointment. On her way out, this gal asked if Laura might know of a homeschool mom who was perhaps older with a couple kids. This mom, Teri, had a boy around ten years of age, a girl around fifteen, was just starting her homeschool journey, and needed help. Laura had thought of me. Casey and Kelcy were right in that age range, and I was an older homeschool mom, fifty-four years old at that point. Laura asked me if she could give this mom my phone number. It was fine with me.

A couple days later, Teri called. She was just delightful. She came to my house so we could meet. I gave her homeschool ideas and showed her what we did. When she walked in the house, I was embarrassed because I had just taken every picture off my walls, which were painted a bland white, as I was trying to figure out how to make my home look warm and inviting. I can do a lot of things, but I don't have any gift for interior design. I just didn't know what my style was or how to find it.

Teri immediately told me that she had a gift for interior design and she would love to "pay me back" for my help with homeschooling by helping me with my house. I accepted! She looked around at all our farm stuff, took a look out in the barn for old farm things there, and told me she had a great feel for my style already. She had just the things needed to decorate our home in the best way. We began the process, and Teri was amazing in that she did it at virtually no cost–from choosing paint colors to furniture placement, pictures on the walls, carpets, and more, using everything we already had. And I loved it all!

Teri gave me many great tips on home decorating. She helped me realize my own style and finally, after twenty years, I was truly comfortable in and loving every room of our home. As a result, when the time came to furnish the Airbnb house, I was ready! I knew the colors that would work to create a warm and comfortable space. I knew the style I wanted and had learned how to place the furnishings we had. And we had plenty of furniture and décor.

Much of what we had came from others we had given to and cared for in the past. We had couches, loveseats, futons, beds, dining room tables and chairs, dishes and cutlery, pots and pans, microwaves and mini-fridges. Much of it came from many of the international students we had helped move and supplied household goods to over the years. We had plenty of great southwest style pictures from my dad and mom's collection. We had lamps, dressers, rugs and TVs from friends who we had helped previously with their needs. We had lots of household items from Clint's mom, aunt and uncle. We were set and greatly blessed.

The Deardorff house Airbnb opened up and took off. We were amazed at how it stayed very active even through the winter. It was a blessing for us financially as well as for me, keeping me centered and steady with scheduling, cleaning, and taking care of this new business we had.

THE 2020 GIVING YEAR

My sweet dad died on February 23, 2020. My dad had become my top priority from 2014 on. To keep him safe and loved through his last years was where I put my energy. It was a long haul and, frankly, emotionally draining and sometimes physically exhausting as we navigated all the changes pertaining to him. He was on hospice for over three years—longer than any hospice patient the local hospital had ever had. I'm so thankful they stuck with me to walk the journey. They were awesome in their support of me and dad.

There were many times I knew that dad was living in the blessing of the Lord because of his heart for God throughout his life and his being a giver and tither for the long haul. His journey finally came to an end and he graduated to heaven at the age of ninety. It was a huge blessing that he passed away right before COVID-19 hit the planet. We were able to be with him and say our goodbyes, sing his favorite hymns with him, and bless him as he left. It was a precious time.

Financially, his accounts were full, enough to bless his children and his children's children. *"A good man leaves an inheritance to his children's children,"* (NKJV) Proverbs 13:22a says, and this was exactly what my dad did. When he moved up from New Mexico in 2005, he didn't have enough for himself and my mom to live in residential care facilities if that were to be needed for more than a few months, but through wise financial planning and management over fifteen years, his accounts had grown. We had worked with him extensively, introducing him to Dean, our financial planner, and my frugal dad had prospered.

I was excited about all the giving I would be able to do after the money was split and transferred to my sister, brother, and me. But then Coronavirus hit and the stock market began dropping like a stone, day after day, week after week. It was truly disheartening. Finally, in April, we were able to get all the legal work done. The inheritance was released. By then it had lost at least a third of its value, but we "monitored and adjusted," as my dad liked to say, and re-invested the portion we had received.

By April, we were deep into the Coronavirus lockdown and all Airbnbs in our state were shut down completely, so no income was coming there. In spite of that, God began to emphasize in my heart to give, and give BIG. I kept sensing His gentle push toward giving. So the giving began. In a two-month period, May and June 2020, Clint and I gave over $36,000 to missions, to friends, to ministries, to young couples to pay off school costs, and to young families to start up college accounts for their young children. These are some of the gifts:

- When I was in Romania in summer 2019, the Romanian family running the YWAM base there were moving into their first house and had asked for financial support. We gave $6,000 to complete the stairs in their new home.

- We helped a BSSM student get back from the U.S. to her family in the U.K. at the end of May since COVID-19 caused major disruptions in air travel with cancellations and price hikes. That amount was around $400.

- We gave to a counseling ministry in the U.K. That amount was $25,000.

- A single widow friend in Ellensburg needed a new car, new iPad, and iPhone as, during COVID-19, they all had died. God had us give her $3,000.

- In June, God led me to attend the same school from Bethel that Kelcy and Casey had attended in person, but I got to do it in their pioneer first online class. God immediately put it on my heart to pay for my student mentor's and her husband's 3rd year tuition–$1,600 total.

All together, the gift amounts were close to $36,000. I knew God had something big in mind with asking us to give so much, especially in a season where lack seemed to be hitting the planet. I kept thinking that something huge must be on the horizon that God knew was coming, and He wanted us shielded and prepared financially for whatever it was. I thought perhaps the world was going to fall apart with COVID-19 and we needed to have a secure covering; that was why He was asking us to give extravagantly. Nothing happened in that direction, but what did happen was awesome and amazing and brought us into the awe and wonder of the goodness of God!

LONE PINE LAND SALE

In mid-July, Clint got a phone call from a guy who was interested in buying twenty-seven acres of land we had. We had been working on selling this land for the past several years. It actually was land we had purchased for my dad to live on when he and mom moved to

Washington in 2005. Dad wanted a place in the country, and this fifty-two-acre piece of property, part of the Lone Pine Ranch, became available for $225,000, but my dad didn't want that much land. He couldn't buy the whole piece because he didn't have enough money, and he had no property as collateral on a loan. We were mortgage-free on our own property, so we put that up for collateral and secured a loan for the entire fifty-two-acre piece. We were then able to split it into four parts (nine acres, sixteen acres, eight acres, and nineteen acres). Much like what happened years earlier with Clint's inheritance from his Uncle George and Aunt Thora, this was another 'just before' moment orchestrated by God. Our split of the piece into four parcels took place just before the county law changed that the smallest farm-land could be split into was twenty-acre parcels.

My dad bought the nine-acre piece from us for $75,000. Clint built a house for mom and dad on that property. We kept the rest of the land until 2008 when an acquaintance of Clint's looking for land contacted us and bought the sixteen-acre piece for $200,000. At this point, the land had more than paid for itself. With the sale, we had paid off some of the original loan on the land and put $100,000 into our mutual fund accounts. Within weeks, that $100,000 disappeared on paper (but was still realized in the shares) because of the 2008 market crash. It was disheartening, but we were smart and just let what was left sit. We didn't try to 'play' or 'time' the market.

Within the next couple years, the market rebounded remarkably, bringing us up to the place that we could buy, with cash, our first condo in Redding for Kelcy to live in. Several years later, we bought a second condo in Redding for cash—all because of the growth of our accounts. Again, seeing the hand of God, listening to His voice, knowing when He was putting smart people in our lives, and trusting the process, all brought about great increase.

Through the years, we leased out the rest of the fifty-two-acre property to a farmer for raising hay. By this time, we had two of the parcels left, the eight-acre piece and the nineteen-acre piece. The farmer paid the land taxes and irrigation water for the year, and Clint got some hay for our cattle. It worked pretty well over the years, but in the spring of 2020, the farmer decided he was finished leasing the land. Clint had to scramble to find someone to take over the fields and keep them productive. At this point, it was becoming more of a liability and extra work that Clint didn't need, so we were ready to sell.

We had put up a For Sale sign a couple years before, but even though people were interested in buying, it never worked out. As the years went by, land prices kept going up. Slowly, what started as $300,000 for the twenty-seven acres increased to $360,000. Over winter, our sign blew down and we never got around to replacing it.

But in July, after the two months of our really big giving, a previously interested party called Clint and said he and his wife really had to have the land. He had been interested in buying two years before, but he didn't want to pay the $320,000 we were asking at that time. This summer of 2020, he was more than willing to pay the full $360,000. God made it happen in an amazing way. It closed in September, and the money was put in our accounts. It was a Proverbs 10:22 day! *"The blessing of the Lord makes rich and He adds no sorrow to it."*

GIFTING FAMILIES

There were several exciting things to me about this land sale. The first was we could finally pay off the Deardorff Airbnb house mortgage after two and a half years. We were again debt free!

But there had been another dream in my heart from the time Clint's aunt and uncle had given our kids each $10,000 at their births. I wanted to 'pay it forward.' We wanted to do the same for other families with young children who didn't have benefactors like we did. We began with one family from our church by helping them start 529 college accounts for their kids. We had started this several years prior by dropping in $1,000 per year for each of the two children on their birthdays. With the land sale, we were able to bring both of their kids' accounts up to the $4,000 level.

We then felt led to pick out two more families with children in the baby through four-year-old range, help them start 529 accounts through our financial advisor, and set their accounts at $5,000 per child. It was a wonderful feeling to be able to bless these families in this way, knowing that it was a good start for their own kids' futures. We look forward to increasing those amounts to $10,000 per child at some point while also keeping an eye out for other families to bless.

Also, with the land sale, we were able to pay off two student loans totaling $14,000 for a young college student, as well as give to another friend who was struggling financially in the middle of a painful marital separation.

Again, the sense from God came for giving. This time He was putting on our hearts to remember the poor, that the poor should be the next focus of our giving for the coming season. It is important enough to Him to be mentioned in the scriptures many times. The poor are near and dear to His heart and He notices when we give to the poor as seen in Proverbs 19:17, "*Whoever is generous to the poor LENDS TO THE LORD, and he will repay him for his deed.*"

Soon after I had this sense that this should be our next area of giving, I opened up my social media account and saw a post from a friend of thirty-five years. Actually, this gal was one of the high school girls I had mentored when I was doing children's ministry in Albuquerque all those years ago. She had started a ministry in New Mexico called New Mexico Dream Center (https://www.nmdreamcenter.org/). They work with homeless and trafficked youth. The invitation from God to support this ministry was strong, and so we gave.

Things like this can seem circumstantial when a thought flits across my mind or an image stands out to me. But I have learned that God likes to be hidden sometimes, to do things in a covert way, to call us to the greatness He has for us by making us seek Him out. Bethel Church calls Him 'Jehovah Sneaky' in times like this. I have also learned that He speaks in many, many different ways, and it pays to be aware of His subtle signals.

If I lean into these unusual 'coincidences' and ask God if this is Him, I will usually hear His voice. I learned this at our first summer worship school at Bethel. Dan McCollam, a special speaker and minister from Vacaville, California, spoke about this very thing. It was an amazing learning experience for me. He told us that if, when these types of unusual things happen, something may just look a little different, feel odd, and it catches our attention, instead of saying or thinking, '*Oh, that's just probably me, but it could be God*', flip it around and say, '*It could be me, but it's probably God.*' Dan said that if we would do just that one simple thing, we could hear from God at least 60% more.

Well, that was definitely something I wanted and I began doing it. I was amazed at how often I was hearing God share His heart with me, how He speaks in so many different ways, always trying to get my attention turned to Him. I am still discovering His purpose in that–sometimes just because I'm His friend and He loves sharing His thoughts with me, sometimes to bring hope, healing, or deliverance to someone, and sometimes to even heal me of some sadness or wound I had long forgotten. He's just that good!

Chapter 7

A NEW SEASON

In looking back through my journals as I have been writing this book, I have seen and felt the strength of my desire to change the world, to give something substantial to the people I am in relationship with. In whatever way I can, I want to empower everyone I know to have a focus, a relationship, and many encounters with God. There have been seasons when this has burned in me with a white-hot-fire intensity.

There have been other busy seasons, during the years of raising and homeschooling our kids, or during the years of caregiving my dad, where the feelings of intensity faded. There have even been some seasons where I was completely discouraged that everything God had built in me was gone and I would never be used again by Him, or that I would have to start over completely. I have recently wondered if I would even have the energy and drive needed to start again with new relationships, new mentorships, or new challenges and mountains to climb and conquer. But I have seen that God always has used every season of my life to build something in me for the next.

I really miss the worship nights we had in the upstairs shop room, the community that developed, the blessing of God's presence, love, and grace with so many American and international college students.

The season for weekly get-togethers to worship ended as my dad's care needs increased. Our core group of college students left to go back to their countries or new jobs, and to live their best lives. Even my own kids grew up and left. Sam and Monica left. Casey left. Joseph left. Jack left. Melvin left. And I found I just didn't have the energy to try to keep it going. Also, the international student population at CWU shifted. Fewer students were coming. Our co-leader and wonderful lover of international students, Kent, retired from teaching at Central Washington University, which left him out of the loop at the university. This cut our international student population significantly. And then, of course, COVID-19 hit where everything was shut down.

But there is always the remembering of what God has done. Throughout the Old Testament, God told the Israelites to set up altars as places of worship and to remember God's covenant and what He had done for them. They set up stones of remembrance so they could give their children a history of God in their nation, their lives, and remember His glorious promises (Joshua 4:20-21). I learned about these altars as a young child, and I always loved them. I began making my own altars, not so much by setting up stones and offering sacrifices, but through writing down encounters with God in my journals, through sitting down at the piano and singing songs of my childhood and growing-up years to Him, and even through writing this book.

I have those cherished memories of my own, but I recently discovered others have God-memories that include me too. Here is one.

DO YOU REMEMBER THE TIME?

In the fall of 2020, a Seattle friend, John, visited us. He and his wife were moving to Idaho and needed to spend the night before traveling on. They had lived in the flight path of SeaTac Airport for twenty-seven years, had just sold their house, and were on the move. As we were catching up, John reminded me of something that happened in 2007.

We had been visiting them at their home in Seattle. The neighborhood was doing poorly, becoming run down as neighbors left their properties to decline. Neighbors' yards had trash and garbage bags piled high, which invited rats and other vermin to infest the neighborhood. John had said that the neighborhood was going downhill fast. There was no way they would ever be able to sell the house and move if they wanted to.

He reminded me that when he said that, I hadn't agreed with him. In fact, I had told him that did not need to be the case. And I prayed right then for a turn-around, for increase and blessing on their neighborhood. The next year, 2008, the economy and market crashed which caused many of the surrounding families to have to move out of the area as they couldn't afford their homes any longer. Others moved in and began fixing up the properties. The turn-around came and this year, thirteen years after that moment … thirteen years after releasing faith for a breakthrough and a better neighborhood for our friends, John was able to sell his property at top dollar.

When I hear confirmations like this of something I had heard from God and then stepped out on, it strengthens my faith to move out more, to have no fear or hesitation when I sense God calling or leading me into something. I love seeing His hand touch people around me when I move as He moves. One of my student mentors this last term in my BSSM Online course said this of me:

> *"Something . . . I've seen through you is that you are so confident in moving with the Lord and partnering with the Lord. You are like, He's on this and I'm doing it."*

I just loved it when she said that because it again confirmed to me that God not only loves me, but He likes me. He likes what He created in me. I am good at partnering with Him!

GIVING DURING A SHUT DOWN

This has been a strange shut-down year of COVID-19 from March 2020 through these current early months of 2021. The following is a recently added declaration prayer that I have been saying over myself and my family. Throughout this year, I have been hearing God's voice and we have been walking and living in His abundance. We have been extremely blessed and covered by His hand as we have been obedient to His leading. This prayer was posted by Shawn Bolz either on his website (https://bolzministries.com/) or in one of his podcasts, I can't remember. But either way, it is a powerful declaration and truth in our lives.

> *"Father God, I am living an "anything can happen" life. Thank you, Lord, for making that possible. Thank You for helping me partner my faith with Your ability. Thank You for helping me walk in a life filled with heaven's economy—fully resourced and fully providing resources. I am a child who lives in abundance, giving resources to the world around me. In Jesus's name. Amen."*

Out of this declaration and throughout this year, we have continued to give. Because of the land sale and other increase God brought us in 2020, we have been able to lift our normal giving to the $1,000 level and beyond.

God opened up another stream of income to us this fall through a very unexpected source. In the summer a gal, Jennifer, was moving into town for a physical therapist job. She stayed in our Airbnb for a few weeks. As she was looking for a cheaper apartment to rent once she settled in, I mentioned we had a couple empty apartment-type rooms at our place. We live seven miles out of town, and we made the spaces available to her if she was interested. She decided to rent in town but began passing on our name to others. As a result, we have rented to two young adults who were here in the valley for short-term jobs, and we've acquired one wonderful long-term renter. This has opened up even more opportunity to give and be connected to others who God wants us to be in relationship with.

A DIFFERENT TWIST ON GIVING

Throughout my recent giving journey, I have encountered a number of folks, mostly women, who really, really want to give more than their budgets and households will allow. God gave me an idea to begin giving them 'seed for sowing.' I thought if I could give others $100 now and then to find someone who God wanted them to give to, it would be serving a dual purpose. The money God had given us would be meeting the needs of people we would probably never meet, and it would give these givers a chance to hear from God specifically and have the opportunity to give without limitation.

This was another idea inspired by Robert Morris, the pastor at Gateway Church. He began to see that when he gave monetary gifts to people, they were very grateful and expressed their thanks to him. Robert became aware there were many times he took the credit for the gift he had given and enjoyed receiving the thanks, but all the thanks belonged to God as it was all His in the first place. Robert realized that just having a desire TO give comes from the heart of God. It is His goodness that causes us to want to give.

Robert decided to change things up by using others to give gifts to an intended recipient, instead of giving the gift personally. This removed him from being seen as the benefactor. Also, when he did give a gift himself, he began to tell the recipient, "*Someone gave me this to give to you.*" He found acknowledging God as the giver was a much more satisfying way of giving. He felt the pleasure of the Lord on this way of giving.

I have been able to do this type of giving several times in the past few months, and it has been exciting to see how God has opened up opportunities to give for us without us even knowing the recipients. It has been beautiful to see how the givers have been hearing God's voice in who to give to and when to give. It is like a scavenger or treasure hunt for them to lean in to hear who the next person is to receive God's blessing. It always opens a door to share the love of Jesus to others.

ANOTHER STREAM

We have also launched another giving stream in this season that is really exciting. In the fall of 2020, when we were able to pay the mortgage completely for the Airbnb house, we were now in a place of having no debt. The idea began forming in my heart that it would be amazing to be able to give ALL the income above the basic monthly expenses of the house. It would be another step towards the fulfillment of my dream to give 90% and live off the 10% like R.G. LeTourneau. Clint and I talked about it, prayed about it, and came into agreement to give it a shot for six months, then re-evaluate.

So the giving has begun! It has been so exciting to see God fill the house with travelers, which in turn fills the account with "seed for sowing." So far, because of the Airbnb income, in the first three months of this year, we have been able to give support to our Romanian YWAM family friends, give money for room and board to three struggling BSSM international students, buy four very needed baby cribs and mattresses as well as three $100 gift cards for mothers who come into our local CareNet ministry, and give support to a missionary in Mozambique, Africa to buy food for the children in her orphanage.

We really believe what Jesus said about generosity and have seen God at work in our giving. Years ago, a pastor taught us from Luke 6:38, *"Give, and it will be given to you. A good measure, pressed down, shaken together and running over, will be poured into your lap. For with the measure you use, it will be measured to you"* (NIV). He used an illustration where he brought out a wheelbarrow, a shovel, and a spoon. He showed how you can give by the spoonful, the shovelful, the wheelbarrow, even the truckload and larger. All those amounts of giving will receive back in the same measure, because this is the way the earth is designed—sowing and reaping is built into the planet and will always take place. A key is the size of the measure you give with. Many people give, but at the teaspoon level, then complain and are confused when they don't see much increase at all. They never graduate up to the next level of giving. We have found that the truth in this verse is solid. As we have given in greater and greater measure through the years, as we have set the bar higher and higher each year of our giving, the measure we measure out has definitely come back in abundance.

Another key is perseverance. Just as an acorn doesn't become an oak tree overnight, what we sow will grow and bring a harvest if we don't give up. We need to be ready to be on this giving journey for the long haul. We shouldn't be concerned when we don't see immediate results, but remember that many of God's promises to the faith-filled people in the Bible took time, sometimes many years, to come to pass. A scripture we have turned to when we seemed to be in a dry time is Ecclesiastes 11:1, *"Send your grain across the seas, and in time, profits will flow back to you"* (NLT). There will be a return, there will be more seed for sowing and abundance for living, if we are patient and persistent.

What a great way to live! It does cause others to scratch their heads and wonder how and why we give like we give, but it is so worth it to see the Kingdom of Heaven expanded and Jesus get His full reward!

IN CONCLUSION

It is now a new season for me. My assignment with my dad has ended and I'm not completely sure what is next. But I hear God saying to just wait and keep doing the things I am doing. Keep giving, keep sowing. Keep enjoying what He has given me, including BSSM-Online to rest in, surrounded by prophetic people who are such a loving community.

I know that there have been so many seasons in my life where it seems like everything had ground to a halt, everything that I was moving toward and in with passion had seemed to have died . . . BUT GOD! He has always started it all up again in a different form, a different place, a different path.

In the fall of 2020, I was given a prophetic word by the Revival Group Pastor in my BSSM-Online class. That day in our Zoom small group, we were told to give words to one other person in the group without knowing who it was. This was certainly a stretch for me. We had each been assigned a number, and after we gave what we felt God was saying to that person, we were told who the word was for. It was truly amazing how God worked in each of us to have the specific word, gentle encouragement, and hope that each person needed. That day, our Revival Group pastor attended (via Zoom) our small group, even though he wasn't a regular member. He was given a number, too, and as he began to give what he felt the Lord saying, it was abundantly clear to me and others in the group that this word was for me! Here it is:

Prophetic Word 10/7/2020 Small Group

"I immediately heard the word Golden, then I SAW a picture of a golden egg. Then as I watched, the golden egg started rolling down a hill – away. I started asking questions of God. Automatically, typically I would think a golden egg means finances. But as the egg went down the hill, it got bigger and bigger – important to note that. As I asked God about it, He said the egg represents something that has been birthed, something that's been sat on, dreamt about, and it's at that stage where it now IS – the chicken laid the egg and there it is. Great. It's been produced for a while, here it is. It is something about the dream that this person cares immensely about.

And then golden does not necessarily pertain to finances at all, but actually more a sense of it is to be handled with that kind of care. It's like if I give my wife a gold bracelet or a silver bracelet—now in one sense, it shouldn't matter because it's a gift and they should both be held. But I know that if there is a higher monetary value, there is a desire to take care of that thing, whatever it is . . . that's just an illustration.

Then there's a sense of it being gold wasn't necessarily about finance but it is more about the sense of care and the way it was supposed to be handled. And then as it rolled away and got bigger, I noticed that as I was watching it, there was no fear. There was no anxiety. There was no sense of, "Oh my gosh this is getting away." So I started asking, What's that about?

And it was like Oh, the dream that you've handled with care is at a place now where it has gained momentum and I just wanted to release over you that those things that you have been dreaming of that seemingly look as though they are getting away from you is actually that you've handled them so well that they've gained momentum. And in order for it to grow into what God has in mind, it needs to get further away from you. Not that you don't have anything to do with it, but it needs more space. So I'd be looking for people to partner with to help see that dream come to fruition."

I look at this word from time to time to revisit it and ask God for more clues as to what it all means. I do think that it has to do with the financial journey Clint and I have been on. I believe it has to do with launching our own children into their adulthood and destinies with

God as well. I know there is more because God always has layers that
need to be unpacked in what He is telling us. I am confident that I
will know what I need to know in His time.

The word did remind me of Isaiah 54:2-6 (NASB 1995), a passage that had been one of my go-to passages during many times of
waiting in my life:

'Enlarge the place of your tent;

Stretch out the curtains of your dwellings, spare not;

Lengthen your cords

And strengthen your pegs.

'For you will spread abroad to the right and to the left.

And your descendants will possess nations

And will resettle the desolate cities.

'Fear not, for you will not be put to shame;

And do not feel humiliated, for you will not be disgraced;

But you will forget the shame of your youth,

And the reproach of your widowhood you will remember
no more.

'For your husband is your Maker,

Whose name is the LORD of hosts;

And your Redeemer is the Holy One of Israel,

Who is called the God of all the earth.

'For the LORD has called you,

Like a wife forsaken and grieved in spirit,

Even like a wife of *one's* youth when she is rejected,'

Says your God."

These verses I held fast to during the years I was waiting and be-lieving for marriage and family. God did fulfill the desire of my heart in giving me both of those. Then He expanded my heart in giving me the nations to bless and cherish during our international student years with Friday Night Worship Nights, cooking classes, and fall farm par-ties. Now He has given me a new twist on these verses and He is in the process of bringing me many others to give to and bless financially.

I love how God continues to bring opportunities to give and to serve into each of our lives. Even as I am coming to the end of this book, we have an opportunity to do some more giving–a surprise gift to one of the leaders in my BSSM-Online course as we finish the current term.

I was leaning into Holy Spirit to see what would be good to give. I thought of my teaching year in Tucson, Arizona and the generous cash gift the families of the students gave my co-teacher and me at the end of the year. I realized that now I am having the opportunity to "pay it forward." I was so grateful for the $350 dollars and remembered how much I needed it. I had no savings, was living month-to-month, and not doing well managing my meager salary. But God! He was teaching me and training me for my future of extravagant, radical, and abun-dant giving. He was showing me that I was worth His investment in me. I had a glimpse into His heart and how He uses others to bring His blessing. He was blessing me simply because He loved me and wanted me to feel and know His extravagant love. He was showing me that, in spite of all my questions about my personality, my value, and my worth for years and years, He saw me as a valuable treasure and He was working in my life. He had not forgotten me.

I read someplace recently that big testimonies come as we grow our faith through the small things of life, as we demonstrate our willingness to listen to the Holy Spirit and follow wherever He leads. It is all about our relationship with the Holy Spirit.

I pray that these words I have written are used by God to ignite courage and faith in every area of life, but especially in the area of abundant and extravagant giving. God is not a respecter of persons (Acts 10:34; Romans 2:11). My prayer is that the stories we have of increasing the measure of our giving inspire you and give you hope that you can get there too, if it is the desire of your heart, as it has been mine. What He has done for us, He will do for anyone. We truly believe and have seen that, if you steward what has been given you, and steward it well, God will give you more.

> "*Now He who provides seed for the sower and bread for food will provide and multiply your seed for sowing [that is, your resources] and increase the harvest of your righteousness [which shows itself in active goodness, kindness, and love]*"
> 2 Corinthians 9:10 (AMP).

REFERENCES

Bach, David. *Smart Couples Finish Rich.* Crown Publishing, 2002

Baker, H.A. *Visions Beyond the Veil.* Whitaker House, 1950

Day, Edward Warren. *One Thousand Years of Hubbard History, 866 to 1895: From Hubba, the Norse Sea King, to the Enlightened Present.* CreateSpace Independent Publishing, 2010 (Reprint)

Deshazo, Lynn. "More Precious than Silver," Track 3, *More Precious Than Silver,* 1982, Integrity Hosanna! Music, CD.

Hughes, Ray. *Facebook,* October 12, 2020. https://www.facebook.com/selahthunder/posts/10157288052341022.

Johnson, Bill. *When Heaven Invades Earth.* Treasure House, 2003 (p. 136)

McMillen, S.I. and David E. Stern. *None of These Diseases.* Fleming H Revell Co., 1984

Metzger, Bruce. "Jesus and Others and You." 1951

Nee, Watchman. *The Normal Christian Life* Tyndale House: Carol Stream, IL 1977

Savelle, Jerry. *In the Footsteps of a Prophet.* J. Savelle Publications: Crowley, TX 1999

CPSIA information can be obtained
at www.ICGtesting.com
Printed in the USA
FSHW021413050821
83849FS

9 781737 359708